Casey Stengel

A Biography

By Norman MacLean

DRAKE PUBLISHERS INC.
NEW YORK   LONDON

Published in 1976 by
DRAKE PUBLISHERS, INC.
801 Second Avenue
New York, N.Y. 10017

Library of Congress Catalog Card Number: 75-36157

MacLean, Norman
    Casey Stengel.

New York   Drake Pub. Inc.
April 1976   1. Baseball
              2. Stengel, Casey   I. Title
ISBN: 0-8473-1068-X

B
Stengel

Printed in The United States of America

Contents

CHAPTER 1

The Early Years

Agnes Avenue in the northeastern part of Kansas City, Missouri, was not unlike thousands of similar residential neighborhoods strung out across the United States in the 1880s and 1890s. The streets were quiet, for the most part, and almost universally lined with overhanging elms and oaks. The sidewalks were generally composed of sheets of slate or bricks, if, indeed, they existed at all. The curbstones were primarily designed to keep the horses from trotting up on the front lawn (or even the front porch) and were often the better part of a foot high. Most of the houses were Victorian, with their frames neatly painted and heavily garnished with the ornamental gingerbread of which the builders of post-Civil War America were so fond.

Railroad lines stretching west and east were close at hand and the great moaning sound of the steam whistle pierced the quiet at all hours of the day and night. The streets themsleves were sometimes brick, cobblestone, or plain old dirt pounded down by the hooves of a many a thousand horses.

Into this world Charles Dillon Stengel was born on July 30, 1889, or 1890, depending on your choice of source. The exact year of his birth, like much else about Stengel, was a subject of much speculation as the decades wore on and he rose to national prominence. Some sources even put it at 1891. The most reliable sources, however, place 1890 as the best bet.

As is usual in such cases, there was little in Stengel's early childhood to indicate that he would subsequently become a darling of the television era and one of baseball's premiere managers.

Casey's mother, the former Jennie Jordan, was Irish. His father Louis, was German. He was a businessman who worked for the Joseph Stiebel Insurance Company.

In Stengelese, Casey used to describe his father as "an operator of a sprinkler wagon." Translated, that meant that the Joseph Stiebel Insurance Company was contracted by

1

the city to sprinkle the downtown streets. Most of the roads leading to the downtown area were then unpaved. Great gobs of mud were spread in front of stores and homes by passing horses and wagons and sprinkling helped eradicate the dust, but not much else. And it created more mud.

"Just shows that I was always digging out from mud," Louis had said.

Louis and Jennie had three children: Louise, Grant, and the youngest, Charles. Young Charles was blond and was called "Dutch." He reluctantly studied at Woodland and Garfield grade schools and very happily played baseball on the vacant lots along Agnes Avenue.

Although both Grant and Charles did occasional work on the sprinkling wagon, Charles said, "I wasn't much good at work."

Dutch attended Kansas City's Central High School where he played basketball and football and was elected captain of the football team during his senior year. In 1909 he served also as the left-handed second and third baseman for the baseball team. Usually, lefties are restricted in infield play to first base, because they have to turn to throw to first base. It must not have a handicap, though, since the 1909 Central baseball team won the state title.

The school year book, *The Centralian*, said, "The baseball team was strong in every way, with the feature being the hurling of Stengel." No one else on the baseball team was mentioned.

Stengel suddenly learned that baseball had a commercial side to it. Harzfeld's, a downtown women's store, had a ballteam that played in the Merchant's League. Louis Stengel was a business acquaintance of Sieg Harzfeld, the store owner. Harzfeld took Dutch on at $1.50 per game, the same amount paid to the other players on the team.

When Casey and Edna Stengel returned to Kansas City with the Yankees in 1955, they received a bottle of perfume from the Harzfeld store with a note reminding him that Harzfeld's had been Stengel's first baseball employer.

Dutch Stengel liked to frequent the local pool hall, but he also visited the Olympia Theatre where he could watch the vaudeville shows. His own sense of mimicry was already present and he spent long hours in the theater. For a time Dutch thought he might make some money in the vaudeville circuit. But he also liked the idea of being a professional man and finally figured that dentistry was the right path. And he had the gleam of the idea that he might be able to exchange his pitching talent for tuition and instruments at the nearby Western Dental College.

In the spring of 1910 he reported to the Kansas City Blues for a tryout at their camp in Excelsior Springs, Missouri. Danny Shay, the Blues' manager had him pitch batting practice. The Blues bombed young Stengel's finest offerings and he was soon sent to the outfield as a new member of the team.

Stengel had played only in open fields and the outfield fences gave him trouble. One day Shay yelled to him, after a ball had caromed away off the wall, "Learn to play the angles son."

"If you want somebody to play the angles," growled Stengel, "why don't you hire a pool player!"

Shay did not hire a pool player; he left Stengel behind with two former Major Leaguers, Spike Shannon and Pat Flaherty, who taught him to go back under a fly ball. Still, Shay shipped him out but Stengel did not give up. He joined the Kankakee team in the Northern Association, but the league soon folded. By summer, he was with Maysville of the Blue Grass Baseball League, where he hit a mere .223. Although there is no record of it, he played a few games in September with Kansas City.

Dutch Stengel was a bandy-legged youth, with freckles and large floppy ears. He had started to clown his way through life. In pregame practice he would catch fly balls hit his way and then throw the ball one way and his glove another. Often he would chase after the glove and when nearing it, would slide into the battered piece of leather as if it were home plate. And he was loud, with a clumsy sort of skill.

One of the nearby edifices in Maysville was a local institution for the insane. One of his teammates told Stengel, "It won't be long now before you're leaving us. You're going in there with the rest of the nuts."

That fall he enrolled in Western Dental College as planned. He did all right in school, but he still liked baseball. The next year he played at Aurora in the Illinois-Wisconsin League and was noticed by Brooklyn Dodger scout, Larry Sutton, who also discovered the great Dodger pitcher Dazzy Vance.

Sutton had gone to the game in Aurora by chance. Stengel had had a good day, and his blond hair, freckles, and fighting spirit appealed to the scout. He was to finish the season with a .352 average, which led the league. The Dodgers drafted him for $300.

They assigned Stengel to Toronto, but ordered him to report to Montgomery in the Southern League for training. But, that winter he went back to Western Dental School.

"I was pretty good at making inlays, but I couldn't handle caps. I still shudder when I see an old tin can," he said. "Maybe I wasn't that enthusiastic anymore. My mind was on baseball."

Stengel had one tough session pulling someone's aching tooth. At the college, anyone could come in with a toothache and for free have his problem pulled.

"I wrestled this guy for about ten minutes. I didn't set the chair high enough. He was tall, and finally it looked like I was trying to catch a high line drive, before we decided who was going to keep the tooth, him or me."

The spring of 1912 found Stengel playing left field for Montgomery in their training camp site at Pensacola. In an exhibition game he pulled his first stunt and almost got fired. In pregame practice he noticed a large manhole cover in left field that could be lifted easily. It only went down a few feet. After taking his position when the game started, he lifted the manhole cover and climbed in.

He looked out by lifting the lid up just far enough to see. When the ball came out to left field, the crowd gasped because there was no left fielder.

Stengel explained, "I stood up holding the lid over my head like a shield. But it was heavier than I had imagined, and I staggered around under the load, hoping the ball wouldn't hit me on the head. At the last second I reached out with one hand and grabbed the ball."

The stunt made for good laughs in the ballpark, but the coach was not at all pleased with his performance. He did not repeat the act.

Stengel had picked up the name "Casey" by this time, although even he was not sure how. "Casey at the Bat" was very popular in those days, and that is one source.

"A lot of players were called 'Casey' in those days, and I was from Kansas City. That's 'Kay Cee' shortened down. I think it might have been a bit of both," opined Stengel.

Stengel hit .290 for Montgomery and was befriended by Kid Elberfield, a veteran shortstop who was there after thirteen years in the big leagues. Elberfield told the young man, "forget dental school. You're going up to the Dodgers."

Sure enough, that September, Brooklyn, desperate for some young blood, decided Stengel was what was needed, at least judging from appearances.

Elberfield had more advise for the young man. "Get rid of that straw suitcase. It will fall apart in bad weather. It's only good here in the South. Buy yourself a new one before you go to Brooklyn."

This was the moment Stengel crossed the Rubicon. He had frugally put away $115 for school. A new suitcase would cost $20. Stengel spent the $20 and arrived in New York with $95 in his pocket. On September 11, 1912 he arrived in New York and spent his first evening in the Longacre Hotel on West 47th Street. The next morning began his long journey, via subway and trolley, to Washington Park, Brooklyn, where the Dodgers played.

The gatekeeper would not let him in at first, but Stengel convinced him he was the Dodgers' new outfielder.

"The clubhouse is down there," he said. "And you'd better be good!"

A crapgame was in progress in front of the Dodgers' lockers. Stengel was welcomed warmly by Zack What, and $20 of his hard-earned money had changed hands before he was rescued by manager Bill Dahlen who bellowed, "Are you a ballplayer or a crap shooter, kid?"

Stengel maintained that he was a ballplayer, so Dahlen roared, "Then get out on the field before you don't even have carfare."

Casey started that day in center field. The crowd was sparse, although there was a goodly number assembled across the street in Ginney Flats, where the residents assembled on fire escapes to watch the Dodgers' play. Homeowners rented space there at ten cents a head. A neighborhood bar served beer in big mugs. The crowd was vociferous and loud and very much able to reach the center fielder with its lungs. This impatient panel of critics occasionally speared enemy outfielders with umbrella ribs fashioned to make excellent long-nosed darts.

Stengel made a dream debut with the Dodgers. Against Pittsburgh's Claude Hendrix, he hammered out four straight hits and stole second base. On his last trip to the plate, Fred Clarke, the Pirate's manager, had replaced Hendrix with a lefty, Sherry Smith. He challenged Stengel with, "OK, busher, let's see you cross over, now."

Stengel had never batted right handed, being lefty all the way, but he did so, now, and surprisingly drew a walk.

The next day the papers said the Dodgers had unearthed the new Ty Cobb. "They were to find out I was nothing but the old Casey Stengel," recalled Casey.

A few days later Stengel was ordered to steal second base against the Cubs. The throw beat him easily, but Casey slid hard into the Chicago second baseman, Johnny Evers, trying to knock the ball out of his hand. Evers tagged him viciously and growled, "Try that again, busher, and I'll stick the ball down your throat."

Casey got up, glared at him and snarled, "That's the way I slid in the bushes and that's the way I'm going to slide here. My name is Stengel. Take a good look at me because I'm going to be around for a long time."

Stengel was around a long time, and he outlasted Evers, who became the Cubs' manager the next year. He had arrived in Brooklyn just in time to play in the last National League game in Washington Park, on October 5, 1912, in which the hated New York Giants edged across a run on pitcher Pat Ragon to beat Brooklyn 1−0. There was a crowd of over ten thousand on hand, most of whom knew that it was the end of an era in Dodger history.

Owner Charley Ebbets was in the final process of completing Ebbets Field, which opened in the spring of 1913. Stengel was just what the owner wanted, a new hope for the Brooklyn fans. He had hit .317 in seventeen games, getting eighteen hits and even creaming one home run.

Stengel stories were already infiltrating the Brooklyn press, much to the delight of Casey and the wonderment of his manager Bill Dahlen. One of them concerned his days with Aurora. He had been called out on strikes twice in the same day by an umpire named Arundel. Casey hollered and hollered and Srundel finally laughed, saying, "Yer Out!! Big Shot. Ha, Ha, Ha, Big Shot!!"

"While he was walking at me I was walking back to bench, which was more than 100 feet from home plate. Finally he turned around to get ready for the next batter. I sneaked back on my tip toes, still carrying the bat, and when he bent over the catcher, I unloaded on him with the bat. I was put out naturally and the game was forfeited. I was lucky the league president didn't suspend me or take all my money."

This type of clowning seemed to surprise even Stengel a bit. In high school he had been quiet, even shy. When his high school *basketball* team won the city championship he was asked to talk before the school assembly. He could not do it; he gagged, and sat down.

Casey did not even bring girls to the basketball games because he did not like the remarks of the roughhewn students who attended the games. He was big for his age in high school and was supposed to be a good fighter because he was strong. He was not strong enough for his brother Grant, though, at one time Charles had gotten enough nerve up to ask a certain girl out and he wanted to wear a good pair of shoes. The only ones available were his brother's, which, despite the fact that he was the youngest, were too small for him.

"I cut the tongue off and taped it back on. Still the shoes hurt, but I was determined to go on the date, anyway. I had to leave soon after getting there, because my feet were in agony. I put the shoes back in the closet and said nothing about the torn tongues. A week later my brother discovered them. He yelled to my mother 'Did Charles use my shoes?' She answered, 'No, his feet are too big.'

"But my brother knew and he took a good crack at me, raving, 'I know you wore them. You tore that tongue off.'

"My brother handled me because he would get in the first shot and then start moving. I couldn't catch him. I would get winded and the fight would end," recalled Charles, as his parents always called him. "Grant could have had a big Buick agency, but he only liked to make money when the work was fun. He wound up in the taxi business."

In his youth, Grant Stengel was thought to be the one most likely to succeed as a ballplayer. He was two years older than Charles and both the boys liked to play with all the fellows under eighteen. His father made Grant take Charles along, and they would put him in the outfield or wherever someone did not show up.

"We worked up a trick play with a potato, which I will never forget." related Casey. "One day he played shortstop and I pitched. He took a potato with him. We picked one as near round as possible and he slipped it in his hip pocket. When a runner slid into second after stealing a base, Grant threw the potato back to me. Then when the runner stepped off the bag to take his lead, Grant tagged him with the ball."

One day the boys were literally chased from the ball park, after pulling that stunt, about twenty-five blocks from home. They had to run all the way home. After that, they did not practice their tricks on the other team's home grounds, but at home it was part of the game.

Grant's career came to an end when he was returning from playing with the Armour team in a suburb of Kansas City, Dobson. The team hired a surrey for the trip. On the way home the guys started wrestling and horsing around and Grant fell off the surrey. His foot caught in the brake, sawing off part of his heel.

"There is no doubt that Grant would have made the big leagues, except for the injury. He wasn't a slugger, but he could hit and place the ball and seldom struck out. He could run like a dear and was sharp on the bases. It was the dead ball era and that was what was wanted in the big leagues then. He was a good slider," continued Stengel.

Today with the lively ball, Grant might not have made it. The home run is king and the outfielders play deeper. In Stengel's time, you had to have a good arm to play in the outfield. The outfielders played short and kept men on bases. The idea was to get a man on, advance him to second by stealing or hitting behind the runner, and somehow score him with a single or by getting him to third and then home. Pitchers tried to get hitters to hit fly balls to the outfield. Nowadays that is dangerous and the long fly can become the home run.

Fights started frequently over collisions on the base

paths. When Stengel was compared to Ty Cobb, it was because the Detroit Tiger institution was a great batsman and also a snarling, fighting, base stealer. Stengel, in his debut with Brooklyn, seemed to be this way too.

Left-handed both ways, Stengel was later to thank a certain teacher of his, Mrs. Kennedy, who had insisted on following the rue in Kansas schools that everyone learn to write right-handed. Stengel reached Woodlands Grammar School trying to write left-handed. Mrs. Kennedy, who was not adverse to giving bad boys a couple of switches, kept Charles in class and even stood him in a closet for a half hour on a couple of occasions.

"You remember the tough managers and teachers," laughed Stengel. "I remember John McGraw and I remember Mrs. Kennedy. I write right handed today because of her. When I hurt my arm in the 1913 season, I thought maybe I could even learn to throw righty, but it didn't come to that, as my arm came back."

When Stengel returned home after the 1912 season, he was asked to participate in a special exhibition game. He had undergone a steady bombardment of bean balls in the last three weeks of his 1912 National League debut and was being hailed as the greatest thing in spikes. In nearby Coffeyville, Kansas, Johnson's home town, they were staging a homecoming celebration for him. The National League pitchers had not found Casey's weakness yet, and he was cocky with his .316 average.

"They offered me $15 to play in the exhibition game and I replied that I would play for free to hit against Walter Johnson," said Stengel. "But I took the $15 and then Johnson made me sorry."

Walter struck Stengel out on twelve pitches, only one of which Casey hit, a loud foul down the left-field line.

"The first time up I swung at all three of Walter's pitches. I missed and decided the next time to choke up a bit and just meet the ball. I still missed the ball. I tried to bunt the third time and still struck out. Johnson has twenty-two strikeouts that day and our pitcher Earl Hamilton had nineteen, so it wasn't just me, but I was a Major Leaguer," continued Stengel.

With the fans call of 'Strike Out Casey' ringing in his ears, Stengel forgot about dentistry and decided to concentrate on the National League and the Dodgers. He was to find out that he was not the new Ty Cobb, but he was to earn his spot as a Brooklyn regular—and his resourcefulness and clowning were to make him an unforgettable member of the Dodgers.

Stengel's return to Kansas City was triumphant. In those days being a Major League ballplayer was *the* thing. There was no pro football, hockey, or basketball, and baseball was king. America, especially Mid-America, was a slow-moving pastoral land in which a game such as baseball, with its nuances, stolen bases, and strategical concepts fit perfectly. Stengel, a nonconformist, was sometimes laughed at, sometimes frowned at, but he was ready to spring on stage for America.

His family, although of modest means, was proud of him. His grandfather had emigrated from Germany in 1851, settling in Rock Island at the age of thirteen. Four years later he married Kathrine Kniphals. He died when Louis, Stengel's father, was a mere four.

Casey's mother's family was a bit more illustrious. Jennie Jordan's father was John B. Jordan and her mother was the sister of Judge John F. Dillon, who was on the Iowa Supreme Court and then served on the United States Circuit Court. He also was counsel for some of the big railroads. The Jordans lived in Davenport, Iowa, but when Jennie, a year younger than Louis Stengel, married, the newlywed Stengels moved to Kansas City.

Louise Stengel came along late in 1886, Grant arrived late in 1887, and then came Charles Dillon Stengel. Whether it was 1889 or 1890 does not really matter. Casey Stengel was now a Major League outfielder with the Brooklyn Dodgers—and nothing like that had happened to either the Stengels or the Jordans.

CHAPTER 2

Baptism at Brooklyn

When the 1913 season opened the Dodgers and Casey Stengel moved into a new home—Ebbets Field, then the piece de resistance in modern ball parks. It was not built to be the eccentricity it later became—although its coziness and smallness lent much of the charm for both Dodger players and fans alike.

"It was a neighborhood ball park," recalled Stengel. "I liked it and most of the Dodgers players liked it."

It was constructed under the personal direction of Charles Ebbets, the Dodgers owner and president. Before the start of the 1912 season, with two years left on his lease at Washington Park, Ebbets decided he had had it—began buying up land in the folksy Pigtown district of Flatbush. He finally completed a block bounded by Montgomery Street, Bedford, Avenue, Cedar Place and Sullivan Place.

Ebbets, with the help of Steve and Ed McKeever, owners of a Brooklyn construction company who were given a half interest in the team to complete the costly project, built a steel and concrete ball park. The era of the wooden grand stand was over. It had an ornate entrance known as the Rotunda, which might have stumped a Pentagon expert, but was loved by most Dodger fans.

On Opening Day in 1913 Ebbets Field was minus the left field wall which was to be a Death Valley for left handed pitchers in later years. In fact the left field foul line extended 418 feet 9 inches before it came to the wall. Duke Snider may have felt hemmed in, in center field with the famous bleachers literally hanging over him, but Zach Wheat, the Dodgers hero at the time, didn't and neither did Stengel.

The Dodgers fans looked forward to the new season, with their new ball park and their new-hot shot rookie, Charles "Casey" Stengel. They were in for some surprises with both.

In a pre-season exhibition game someone forgot to bring the key to unlock the bleacher seats. Hell hath no fury

like a Dodger fan denied admission to his plank in the
bleachers. When the bleachers sold out for an important
game in 1916, Dodger fans dismantled a telegraph pole and
using it as a battering ram, forced entrance into the
bleachers.

The original stands were double decked from the right
field corner on Bedford Avenue around to just past third
base on the Cedar Place side. They met there to form a concrete bleacher section which extended to the left field wall
on Montgomery Street. Right field was always short and
never exceeded more than 301 feet. Most of the park's history it was 297 feet and was topped by the famous high
screen, which didn't exist in 1913, Stengel's first full season
with the Dodgers. In the beginning, center field was a
whopping 467 feet 9 inches from the plate. It gradually
crept in until in 1957 when the park saw its final baseball,
the barrier was only 389 feet.

William Dahlen was in his fourth and last season of
suffering with the Superboys as the Dodgers were sometimes known. He knew that Stengel wasn't the new Ty
Cobb, but he hoped to erase some of the faults which he
saw in Casey. The fans, happy with the new park, came out
347,000 strong. That was a pretty solid increase over the
243,000 for the last year in Washington Park.

Stengel, having trouble with spit ball pitching, which
was then both legal and prevalent in the National League,
hit .272 in 124 games. He hit seven homer runs and knocked
in 44 runs.

He worked hard perfecting the carom off the right field
wall and was rated as the Dodgers right field regular. The
concrete wall was a rarity in those days and the Dodgers
had an advantage in that rival outfielders were used to playing balls on the carom off much deader wooden fences.
Stengel became adept at playing the carom, oft times prac-
ticing for hours with three fuzzy looking balls which almost
had the covers worn off.

The Dodgers finished sixth, winning 65 and losing 84
games. The Giants, across the river, won the pennant under
John McGraw. They won 101 games and lost 51. Charlie
Ebbets was unhappy and even though Stengel had started
to emerge as a bit of character, Bill Dahlen was doomed.

Casey showed up one day for batting practice with a

STENGEL SWINGS THE BAT FOR BROOKLYN.

large sign, reading "My name is Charles Dillon, 'Dutch' Stengel. Would you please allow me to go up and hit in batting practice?"

Ebbets fired Dahlen after the season and installed Wilbert Robinson, who was to manage the Dodgers from 1914 through 1931. In time the team became known as the Robins, after their zany manager.

Despite his image as the leader of a bunch of clowns, Robinson was a smart manager. He was patronizing at times—and could curse like McGraw. He resented the fact that he couldn't beat his players up as had been done when he was a player. Hence he made up for it with savage attacks of profanity.

Once when Stengel staggered around under a fly ball and finally surrounded it, Robinson said, "If I watch you long enough under fly balls I'm going to have a heart attack."

Stengel worked overtime with Nap Rucker, the great left hander of the Superbas on hitting the spitter. Rucker didn't throw a spitter but he did throw a low sweeping curve which acted like a spitter.

"I got so I could golf at that curve. Suddenly I became fairly respectable at hitting the spitter," remembered Stengel. "It was either that or go back to Kansas City. They almost put me out of the National League with that pitch."

In Robinson's first year Stengel hit .279 with 130 hits, four homers and 56 runs batted in. He played in 126 games. In a pre-season contest at Jersey City, Casey won $50 by catching a greased pig, turned loose amongst the players who had to scramble for the porker.

"I never caught a pig in a poke in my life," said Stengel. "But I wanted that $50.00. But I paid for it later. The other players made me stand in the outfield in foul territory between innings, because of the odor created by the grease. The showers weren't in the ball park and I had to play the whole game. I still think Robinson was in on that."

Another time Stengel's mother visited Brooklyn along with his sister, Louise. Although the Brooklyn fans liked Stengel, they realized he wasn't another Cobb. Dutch couldn't run that fast and had other weaknesses which the NL had ferreted out. He was a "made" athlete more than a natural one—and he wasn't that graceful. When one of the more rapier wits in the crowd let Dutch have it with a crude witticism mother Stengel objected and saying to Louise, "We don't have to listen to this," she left the ball park.

Try as Casey did he couldn't get his mother to return to Brooklyn to watch him play. She didn't understand that the species of fans who inhabit that borough could be raucous, profane and loving all in a few seconds.

The Dodgers hadn't won a pennant since before the turn of the century, but the 1915 team was beginning to flex its muscles. "Next Year" that famous Brooklyn battle cry was just around the corner. In Robinson's second season Casey Stengel hit only .237, with 3 homers and 109 hits in 132 games. He was the regular in right field, playing most of the time, but on occasion the left handed hitting Stengel was benched when a left hander was pitching against the Dodgers.

"You can't hit that guy, Dutch," Robinson would say—as he left Stengel's name off the lineup card.

Stengel didn't like it, but years later he remembered how platooning had worked—and he used it when he became the manager of the Yankees and for the first time had the bodies to maneuver with.

In Spring training in 1916 the feeling was that Brooklyn had a chance to win the NL pennant. They had finished fifth in Robinson's first year and third his second with 80 wins and 72 losses. In 1914 attendance had dipped to 122,671 as the euphoria of the new ball park waned. It picked up to 297, 766 a year later and the stage was set for the Dodgers pennant pitch.

The Dodgers were training at Daytona Beach that year, when Ruth Law, a pretty young aviatrix flew over with a salesman from a sporting goods firm and dropped some newly minted golf balls on the beach. Uncle Robbie perked up and claimed, "I bet I could catch a baseball if it was dropped from a plane."

Robbie insisted as his players laughed. "Maybe not from a plane way up, but if one flew from no more than 400 feet I think I could catch a baseball."

"If the ball hit you on the head it would smash your skull and our problems would be over," laughed one player, *soto voce*.

Robbie waxed indignant and took the bait.

"I never got hit on the head playing baseball and I wouldn't get hit if a ball was dropped from a plane."

The big experiment was put into operation. Casey Stengel later denied he had anything to do with later events, but no one ever took his denial seriously. The whole thing smacked of Stengel all the way.

The next day a large crowd gathered on the beach, complete with photographers to record this curious enent. Uncle Robbie put on his catcher's mitt and waited as Miss Law made her run over the beach. In the plane with her was the Dodger trainer Frank Kelly who was picked to be the bombardier for the flight. Kelly didn't bring a baseball, but instead came armed with a large juicy Florida grapefruit.

As the plane soared past Robbie something dropped out. Robbie circled under it and braced his legs for the impact, reaching up with his catchers glove for the "ball." The "ball" grew in size as it hurtled down on the Dodger manager, until it seemed to him to be a great yellow object. It hit his hands and went right through them, seemingly exploding in his face.

The tremendous impact of the grapefruit knocked him flat on his back. He lay in sand, and he lay in the sand moaning, "I'm dead. I'm blind. I'm covered with blood. Somebody help me. I'm blind."

The "blood" was juice from the grapefruit and the juice had made him unable to see for a short time. The assembled players doubled up with laughter, until finally Robbie opened his eyes and peeked out at his smashed body. He found the blood was grapefruit juice, and the ball nothing more than a large yellow fruit which was now smashed beyond recognition.

Robinson leaped to his feet and blistered the air with profanity, which could be heard all down the beach. For a time it seemed that Stengel's job was in danger. Eventually Kelly was fired by Robbie, who never really forgave him. Stengel's denial of implication fell on deaf ears, but Robinson kept him for the next two years, at least.

"If that had been a baseball I would have caught it," insisted Robinson. "And I know Stengel thought that gag up."

The Dodgers got off fast, and despite a 26 game win-

STENGEL WITH THE BROKLYN DODGERS IN 1914.

ning streak by the hated Giants in September, Brooklyn
won the pennant. Next year had arrived in the Borough.
Stengel hit .279 in the season, with 129 hits, 8 home runs
and 53 RBI. In the World Series the Dodgers fell before the
Boston Red Sox, but Stengel hit .364. He didn't play in one
of the games that a young left hander named George
Herman Ruth pitched.

"Uncle Robbie knew I couldn't hit that left handed
fella named Ruth. You know something," said Stengel,
years later. "He was right."

The Red Sox beat the Dodgers four games to one, but
Brooklyn had won the NL pennant and boomed their attendance at Ebbets Field to a whopping 447,747. Even Charley
Ebbets was happy, although still beset with financial
problems left over from building the new ball park.

When Stengel reported for Spring Training in 1917 the
clouds of World War I had drifted to this side of the Atlantic. Casey didn't know it, but he was playing his last year
for the Dodgers.

"I have always felt proud that I played for the Dodgers
first pennant winner," said Casey. "They were paying me
peanuts and I thought I was worth more, but I loved playing
in Brooklyn."

Stengel did pretty well in 1917, playing in 150 games,
the most in his career in the NL, but his average slipped to
.257. He hit 6 homers and had 69 runs batted in, also a
career high. And he got 141 hits, the most in his entire time
in the Majors.

But Charlie Ebbets and Stengel were to clash and
Casey was playing his last year in Brooklyn. In his time
with the Dodgers, Stengel led a fast life off the field, too. A
bachelor, at the time, he became the ring leader of a group
of six roisterers. They frequented a certain Brooklyn
saloon wherein the bartender tired of listening to them gripe
about Uncle Robbie, the Dodgers, the umpires, and the
world in general, finally nicknamed them, "The
Grumblers."

After a lost ball game one evening, the Grumblers
tangled with some fans who were needling them. The incident caused a furor in the press, and Ebbets came into the
dressing room the next day and upbraided Robinson for let-

BABE RUTH PITCHED AGAINST CASEY DURING THE 1916 WORLD SERIES.

ting his players get out of hand, and his players for banging around some of the paying "Faithful."

Robinson backed his players, telling Ebbets, "The guys didn't do that much. Mr. Ebbets." Turning to Stengel, he asked, "You and Jeff Pfeffer weren't drinking as much as Mr. Ebbets claims, were you, Casey?"

"Of course not," said Stengel. "We only had four apiece."

"Only four glasses of beer," checked Robinson.

When Ebbets had left, Robinson roared, "I bet those glasses were as big as cookie pots, weren't they?"

Stengel and Ebbets locked horns over his salary with Charley, saying, "I need your help to pay for the ball park."

Stengel reminded, "With the amount of money I'm getting I'm too weak to play. I don't get enough to eat."

Stengel was traded to the Pittsburgh Pirates, with whom he promptly got into a similar salary hassle—an acrimonious dispute with owner Barney Dreyfuss. He was sent to the Pirates with second baseman George Cutshaw, for infielder Chuck Ward, and pitchers Burleigh Grimes and Al Manaux.

Stengel had had a $5,000 contract with the Dodgers, but when he reported in 1917 he was sent one with a cut in pay to $3,300. He had the third highest contract on the Brooklyn team, but the management chose not to accept his .364 1916 World Series average, but instead to go with his .257 seasonal average. Stengel held out, sent back the contract and claimed it was the bat boy's deal. Ebbets sent another contract back, this time with a $2,300 cut, from the previous document of $5,000.

Stengel reported out of condition in 1917, when he finally accepted part of the cut. In his first at bat he hit a triple and then pulled a muscle sliding into third base. He was out of the lineup for a while and finally had what he admitted, "was a bad year, even though they used me more and the figures were higher, except the average."

This cost him when he was traded to the Pirates, as Dreyfuss based his offer for 1918 on his Dodger contract and Stengel's record in 1917.

Dreyfuss offered him $3,000 and Stengel held out for

$4,000. He finally got his price, but neither he nor Dreyfuss was satisfied with the whole thing. One day Stengel misjudged a fly ball in right field and came under the ire of the Pirate fans nearby. He used his old Brooklyn ploy about not having enough to eat. Dreyfuss heard about it and determined to get rid of Stengel.

Before he left the Pirates, Stengel perpetrated his famous sparrow trick on the fans at Ebbets Field. It happened on June 6, 1918 when the Pirates came to Brooklyn for the first time since Stengel had been traded.

As expected the Brooklyn fans gave Stengel, their former hero, a rough going over. They still liked Stengel, but he was wearing a Pirate uniform and that made him an enemy. Casey understood and had no animosity. But he had the answer, although it required the use of a prop, in this case a sparrow.

When he came to bat, Stengel swung three big bats over his head and made menacing gestures at the Brooklyn pitcher. As he stepped into the batters box, he bowed from the waist and turning to the grand stand tipped his cap. Out flew the bird. Stengel had turned the tide and had given the Dodgers Faithful the bird before they gave it to him.

The crowd loved it, but Dreyfuss didn't see the humor.

"I got three hits that day," said Stengel. "They said I wasn't serious, but I think that the other players who didn't get three hits with no sparrows in their hats weren't as serious as me. Higher ups are always like that."

Later it was revealed that an old friend on the Dodgers, pitcher Leon Cadore, had given Stengel the bird when he saw it in the outfield. Cadore had been a buddy of Stengel's and he knew what was coming.

"The darn bird kicked up quite a fuss under my cap when it started to come to life under there. I almost couldn't keep it down until I got to bat," recalled Stengel.

"I always knew he had birds in his attic," was Wilbert Robinson's reaction to the whole thing.

Stengel spent most of 1918 in Brooklyn at the Navy Yard. He got into only 39 games before he joined the Navy. Stengel felt his bandy legs weren't ready to march under a full pack. Some genius in the Naval Department decided that Stengel would make a good baseball manager and assigned him to the Brooklyn Navy Yard. He was literally back home in familar surroundings at Fulton Street in the Borough.

"I arranged my own schedule," said Casey. "I made it my business to board each ship as it docked and set up a game for the next day. That way we got them before they got rid of their sea legs. We would still be winning if they hadn't called off that war."

Casey got taken himself once during his Naval managerial tenure. Both teams had to dress in the same dressing room. Because he was reluctant to leave the thirty-seven dollars he had in his Navy Blues, he gave it to his bat boy to be returned after the game. In the bottom of the first inning he looked up and noticed the bat boy wasn't working the bats. Off in the far distance beyond right field he saw something moving in a blur. It was a boy on a bicycle, who looked an awful lot like the bat boy.

"The moral of that story is never trust a boy on a bicycle," said Stengel, who also had to find another boy to handle the chores with the bats, as well as losing his money.

In the 39 games he played Stengel hit .246, "clobbered" one home run and had 30 rbi. Dreyfuss wasn't impressed and Casey and he had another salary squabble. Early in September of 1919 the Pirates got fed up and traded Stengel to the Philadelphia Phillies, which represented Siberia in the NL, in those days. Casey's salary was adjusted and his figures for 1919 weren't bad. They totaled .293 in 89 games with 4 homers and 40 rbi. Stengel wasn't happy with the Phillies. He had become a sore-backed, sore-legged ball player, really incapable of full-time service. But Philadelphia used him in 129 games in 1920 and Casey responded with a .292 batting average, 130 hits, 9 home runs and 50 rbi. Stengel and left-fielder Irish Meusel became fast friends, and were known to break an occasional curfew or two.

But Stengel was a good journeyman ball player, who was to last 14 years in the NL. He played during the era of the changeover from the dead ball to the rabbit. Babe Ruth was being converted from a pitcher with the Boston Red Sox to the Sultan of Swat with the New York Yankees. The NL still played a style of baseball which was based on playing for one run and relying on good defense and a tight

1916 BROOKLYN DODGER OUTFIELD (L TO R) ARE: STENGEL, FRED JOHNSON, HANK MYERS AND ZACK WHEAT.

pitching to hold slim leads, usually one run leads. Robinson and John McGraw, the Giants manager, were expert at the hit and run, sacrifice bunt, sacrifice squeeze, the suicide bunt and such defensive techniques as the cut off and back up of the various bases.

By 1920 Stengel had developed a reputation as a smart, if somewhat zany ballplayer who was something of a rebel and also something of an anarchist. He was a bon vivant off the field and knew all the good watering spots in the National League. And he knew how to get away with breaking curfew.

As a player he was drifting and starting to question the whole business. He hadn't yet decided he wanted to stay in baseball, and thought he had established himself as an NL regular. He hadn't thought much about what he might do after his playing days were over.

Stengel's main forte was rising to the occasion when in a clutch situation or whenever he was in the spotlight. He rarely failed under these types of pressure situations. At 32, or 33, you pay your money and take your choice, Stengel was at a crossroads in his career. He was to go on to the heights as a World Series hero, and at the same time to get a chance to manage, but as 1920 closed he didn't know this, and was blatantly unhappy with his lot with the woebegone Phillies.

CHAPTER 3

Serious Series Hero

By 1921 Americans had begun to figure out ways to subvert the intentions of "do-gooders" who sought to enforce their will on the majority. Most Americans were finding that working around the Prohibition laws could be a lot more fun than having a casual drink at a neighborhood saloon. In fact, many Americans who would never have been tempted to have a go at demon rum were to make their way into the speakeasies. Policemen had a lot which was not a happy one but at least they discovered new ways of enriching their bankrolls. This was done in the best of all possible ways—by *not* doing something, which normally meant finding the speakeasy.

The United States came galloping out of World War I (or the Great War as it was then called, in a highly-energized state and ran at break-neck speed into the 1920s. Tabloid newspapers were making their appearance in the big cities, seemingly for the express purpose of chronicling the bizarre dealings amongst the errant well-to-do. Automobiles, sparse at best before the war, were now commonplace thanks, in large measure, to the assembly-line genius of Henry Ford. The pace of life, especially in the larger cities, was springing forward at a rate heretofore undreamed of.

In this swirling, mad environment was a stage set for Casey Stengel. It was, truly, a stage dominated by the giant figure of Babe Ruth, and Stengel was to play a supporting role. But it was, nevertheless, a role of significance and one in which Stengel was to revel. His innate clown intuitions were never suppressed entirely at any point during his playing days.

Stengel was still the property of Philadelphia during 1921, and he enlivened many an otherwise-dull Phillie contest. Typical of Stengel's influence on the relatively colorless and talentless Phils was the exhibition game the club played in Fort Wayne, Indiana early in the year. Stengel departed from the squad before it left the hotel for the trip to the ballpark and deposited himself in the stands dressed in native farm regalia. As the game began, he started heckling his teammates, "You call yourselves big leaguers?. . . I can play ball better than that . . . " and so forth.

Finally, about the fifth inning, a couple of Phillies came over to where Stengel was sitting in the stands and challenged him to come out on the field. Once out of the stands, they lent Stengel a set of spikes, which just happened to fit him perfectly, and a lefthanded glove. He went on to become the star of the afternoon and was cheered with every move by the locals who, even once they began to suspect they were being put on, enjoyed Stengel's act enormously.

Although Stengel was one of the better ballplayers on the hapless Phillies, his enthusiasm for playing was gradually disminishing as the Phils floundered hopelessly into the depths of the National League's second division. The gradual advance of his age was also a real factor and during the 1921 season, Stengel began to develop backaches. These backaches grew worse as the Philadelphia line slipped steadily lower into the standings. At the time, Stengel was the regular rightfielder for the Phils, and Irish Meusel was the leftfielder. In between these two was Cy Williams, an above-average glove man. Meusel was suffering from a sore arm. The two used to stand in the outfield, both facing Williams, yelling, "Come on, Cy!"

Besides the nagging pain in his back, Stengel had other problems in Philadelphia. His Baker Bowl locker was next to that of manager Bill Donovan. Donovan was a cranky, unhappy man who suffered terribly with the Phillies sad performances. He drove Stengel to distraction with the moans and cries of self-pity after one of the habitual string of Phillie defeats, and Stengel often sought refuge by moving to another locker. Because of his holdout a few years before, Casey's relationship with club owner William Baker was not too good, either. But this circumstance was ultimately to work to Stengel's advantage.

His backaches grew more painful and finally he was sidelined. At this point, Donovan directed looks of reproach and scorn at Stengel at every opportunity and Baker became completely disgusted. More to flee Donovan's pitiful glances than anything else, Stengel mov-

THE NEW YORK GIANTS 1922

JACKSON CVENGROS HIGBEE SHINNERS JONNARD KELLY BURKETT SCOTT
MEUSEL JOHNSON MAGUIRE RYAN HILL J. BARNES V. BARNES ROBERTSON SNYDER
YOUNG NEHF STENGEL JENNINGS McGRAW DOLAN GASTON SMITH FRISCH
McQUILLAN McPHEE BANCROFT BLUME CUNNINGHAM GROH KING RAWLINGS

1922 NEW YORK GIANTS. STENGEL IS SEATED IN SECOND ROW,
THIRD PLAYER FROM LEFT.

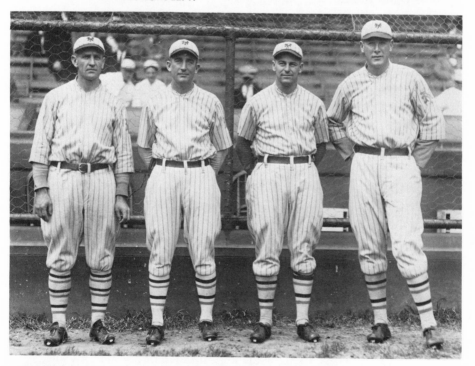

1922 NEW YORK GIANTS OUTFIELD (L TO R) ARE: STENGEL, BILL
CUNNINGHAM, ROSS "PEP" YOUNGS, AND EMIL "IRISH" MEUSEL.

ed to a locker in the back of the clubhouse. One rainy afternoon, Casey was hiding in his rear cubicle waiting the cancellation of the game because of the weather. Club secretary Jimmy Hagan walked into the room and asked, "Where's Stengel?"

Another player responded, "He's dressing back there now."

"Oh, yeah? said Hagan. "Well, he'll be dressing farther away than that after today."

Normally, Hagan was the bearer of news that caused a man to be sent to the minors. Stengel thought the worst, and a hush fell over the clubhouse as Hagan crossed the room and began talking in whispers to Casey. The silence was suddenly shattered when Stengel bolted upright, screamed for joy, and leaped into a dance of celebration. "I've been traded to the Giants!" Stengel hollered.

Stengel hastily pulled back on the uniform he had just been taking off and rushed out of the clubhouse door onto the field in the midst of the still-falling rain. He rushed around the infield, sliding into each base until his uniform was completely soaked with water, dirt, and mud.

He then came charging back into the startled clubhouse, pulled off the uniform, threw it on the floor, and yelled, "Tell that cheap bastard Baker to get this thing cleaned! When's the next train to New York?" His stunned teammates then watched Stengel gallop through a shower, clean out his locker, dress, and race out onto the street still screaming and dancing. "My back's all right, my back's all right," he yelled while running down the sidewalk.

Stengel had been traded by the impoverished Phillies to the Giants with infielder Johnny Rawlings in exchange for a parcel of prospects and Minor Leaguers valued at some $75,000, a substantial amount for the time. The deal had been made by baseball's "Little Napoleon," John (Mugsy) McGraw, the manager who controlled the New York Giants for decades. McGraw, perhaps the greatest manager of his time and one of the greatest in baseball history, had made the deal principally to shore up his bench. He did not expect Stengel to serve as a full-time player. He was also aware of his back problem.

Despite his own disclaimer upon hearing the joyful news, Stengel was suffering from a bad back and did not

STENGEL WITH NEW YORK GIANTS IN 1922.

see much service with the Giants in 1921. He finished the season having appeared in only forty-two games. The Giants won the pennant, their seventh for McGraw since 1902, and defeated the Yankees in the World Series. But Stengel did not even make an appearance in the Series.

None of this, however, dimmed Casey's enthusiasm for playing for the Giants, playing in New York, or playing under McGraw. When he first arrived at the Polo Grounds after the trip from Philadelphia, he walked onto the field and began slapping himself hard all over his body. "Wake up, muscles," he said to himself, "we're in New York now."

Although McGraw was later fond of reminding Stengel that the Giants has spent $75,000 to obtain him, the deal in reality was just one of a series between the two clubs. Adopting a tactic that was made much more famous by their rivals, the Yankees, the Giants had picked out a sagging franchise in their league (the Phillies) and were determined to pluck it clean of whatever talent they could. During 1921, Stengel, Rawlings, Meusel, and pitcher Red Causey were all to go to the Polo Grounds in exchange for the likes of Curt Walker, Butch Henline, Goldie Rapp, Lee King, and John Monroe, none of whom ever became the hottest bubble-gum card in anybody's neighborhood. But the reason for Casey's glee at being freed from Philadelphia was abundantly clear by the continued performance of the Phillies who staggered home dead last, forty-three and a half games to the rear of the champion Giants, with a record of fifty-one wins in 154 games. Donovan was put out of his misery in August, when he was fired by Baker, and replaced by a former pitcher with the appropriate name of Kaiser Wilhelm.

Obviously, Stengel would not have been with the Giants if McGraw did not want him there, but the marriage was indeed a curious one. Stengel was a fun-loving character with a fine ability to live up to his sizable reputation for clowning. McGraw was not especially tolerant of personalities at variance with his own, and he did not particularly find Stengel's frolics amusing.

But McGraw, above all, was a sound baseball man dedicated exclusively to the proposition that the only thing worthwhile about a baseball game was winning it. He felt that Stengel was the type who fit into his strategic needs at the time, and he had dealt for him solely on that basis. McGraw was a hard-liner on discipline who had been bred in the incubator of the fabulous Baltimore Orioles of the 1890s. As a player, he had been a scrappy third baseman but a tough hitter who used every advantage available to defeat the opposition. He managed in much the same way. The 1921 pennant was the first of four in succession McGraw was to guide the Giants home with, a feat that was at that time unprecedented. He was a creative and inventive mind on the baseball diamond, who finally became a dinosaur because of his unwillingness to acknowledge and adapt to the presence of the home run as a primary offensive weapon. Mel Ott, the only power hitter ever developed under McGraw, was really a freak because of his stance and the unique construction of the Polo Grounds.

But added to a more flexible mind, McGraw's basic baseball concepts were more than sound; they were often brilliant. He was a stickler for perfection in the execution of defensive play. During the first quarter of the twentieth century, McGraw was the paramount strategist in baseball. It is little wonder that his thinking had such a profound impact on Stengel and so greatly influenced his own functioning when he finally came into command of a club that had the material to manuever. The platoon system for which Stengel was so noted came from McGraw, who used Stengel as one of the platoon members, alternating him in the outfield with right-handed-hitting Bill Cunningham. In 1922, for instance, Stengel played seventy-seven games in the outfield and Cunningham seventy-one.

It was just for such spot duty that Stengal was acquired. He was to become living proof of the value of the platoon system, but he started with the Giants in anything but a strong fashion. Stengel had appeared in only twenty four games for the Phillies in 1921, because of his back trouble, but he was still hitting a solid .305 for the games in which he did play. For the balance of the campaign, the back kept his playing to a minimum and he hit only .227 for the Giants in eighteen games. Stengel hit no home runs and batted in just six runs between the Phils and the Giants all season. It was certainly not one of his better years, and many a Giants fan wondered what had possessed McGraw to trade a bundle of players for this ex-Dodger eccentric who could not play most of the time and did not do much when he did get in a game.

Giants fans in those days, however, had learned long before not to question the moves McGraw made. They were shortly to have their confidence rewarded. The questions about Stengel's role in 1921 were largely obscured by the fact that the Giants won the pennant and dispatched the lately-successful Yankees in the World Series. Rawlings and Meusel also made important contributions to the Giants effort, so the fans felt they got their money's worth from the dealings with the lowly Phillies. But, in 1922, they found that Stengel was a bargain as well.

Meanwhile, Stengel was getting accustomed to life in the Big City. Despite his previous tour with the Dodgers, Brooklyn was about as far away from New York as China. Brooklyn of the 1920s was still somewhat governed by the rural philosophy of the previous century, and its citizens were rigidly oriented toward their own institutions.

Further, ballclubs in those days, much more so than today, tended to work, travel, and play together. In the Giants, Stengel found many a kindred soul, though few of his compatriots had his *bon vivant* free spirit or his cunning for the effective use of comedy. But the habits of many of his teammates were well matched to his own. The Giants were composed of some outstanding baseball talents like Dave Bancroft, Ross Youngs, and Frankie Frisch. Irish Meusel, a playmate of Stengel's at Philadelphia, helped set the tone for many a soiree that raised cane with manager McCraw's attempts at curfew. The team was well stocked with hail-fellow-well-met companions for these escapades.

The action sometimes even spilled over onto the playing field. Stengel was never notorious as an effective fistfighter, but none could say that his spirit was weak. Well past the age of thirty during his Giants years, Stengel precipitated a near-riot in a game against his former Philadelphia teammates. When Phillie pitcher Phil Weinert persisted in brushing him back, Stengel charged the mound to teach him some respect. Fortunately for all concerned, the police got into the act rapidly and led Stengel away before he suffered serious damage to anything besides his pride. Stengel was a part of the raucous bench-jockeying

STENGEL LEAPS TO MAKE GRAB IN GIANTS OUTFIELD, 1922.

which McGraw encouraged, and he once was punched in the face by Cincinnati pitcher Adolph Luque for his trouble, even though it later developed that Stengel was not the culprit. At least, not that day.

It was once said by one of McGraw's men, "It's great to be young and a Giant." Stengel believed it.

But he wanted to remain a Giant as long as possible and, recognizing that he was in the twilight of his career, he worked hard.

Casey was especially dilligent in preparing himself for the 1922 campaign since it was obvious that his contriubtion to the championship of the previous season was almost nil. He knew that a repeat of that performance or, rather, non-performance, might end his big league career and, certainly, would conclude his stay with the Giants in a hurry.

He arrived at the Giants' spring training camp in the best condition he had been in for several years, probably the best since his release from the Navy. He promptly earned a job or at least half a job, sharing an outfield post with Cunningham. He also got himself into shape for the various extra-curricular activities associated with being a Giant. As he was to say in later years, "When we couldn't find anybody else to fight, we kept in practice punching each other around," much as the later-day Oakland A's were to do. Stengel started one near-brawl in the Giant clubhouse by telling pitcher Jack Scott he would not play centerfield behind him.

"Why not?" demanded Scott.

Stengel, who had as large a pair of ears ever to be separated by a big-league baseball cap, replied, in perfect seriousness, "Your ears are too big. I can't see the ball leave the bat."

Although his combined batting average in 1921 was .284, the bulk of his heavy hitting was done in Philadelphia. Stengel was determined to do better in 1922. He did. As a platoon man, Casey batted a lusty .368 for the Giants and materially contributed to the drive toward their second straight pennant, helping mostly by driving in forty-eight runs on ninety-two hits, a very high production. The Giants had a bit of a struggle with the Reds and Pirates, but they won easily in the end.

The Giants' margin over the second-place Reds was

seven games, nearly double their winning edge of the year before. McGraw drove the club hard, always looking over his shoulder at what his co-tenants in the Polo Grounds, the Yankees, were doing. For decades, the Giants had dominated the New York baseball scene, surviving occasional challenges without serious difficulty. With Babe Ruth now established as the new super hero of baseball, and Miller Huggins, a crafty manager, working on their pitching and defense, the Yankees were a real challenge. In 1920, they had outdrawn the Giants in the Polo Grounds and McGraw had derived great satisfaction from his 1921 Series triumph over them. Such a threat were the Bombers to the Giants domination of New York baseball that the Giants' owners had expelled them from the Polo Grounds effective at the end of the 1922 season. It appeared that the two clubs would again meet in the World Series in 1922 and, when the Yankees survived an unbelievably close race against the St. Louis Browns to take the American League pennant by a single game, they did.

For the first time since 1916, Stengel appeared in a Series. Under the platoon system employed by McGraw, he appeared in only two of the five games played that fall, but he made the most of his chance. In the opening game at the Polo Grounds, Stengel started in center and was one-for-four as the Giants won, 3—2. In game two, he was again the starting center fielder and singled the first time up in the second inning. Then McGraw sent Bill Cunningham, Stengel's alter-ego, in to run for him when the Yankees switched to a lefty. It was his last appearance in the five-game Series, but he was a .400 hitter. Better still, the Giants beat the Yankees without losing a single game. Game two ended in a 3—3 tie after ten innings when the umpires made a disputed termination because of "darkness."

In the ensuing controversy over the umpires' decision, Commissioner Landis ordered the gate receipts from the second game turned over to charity. But the Giants disposed of the Yankees in the next three contests anyway by scores of 3—0, 4—3, and 5—3, making them World Champions for the second straight year.

Stengel celebrated his first World Championship by spending the winter of 1922-23 in California. Irish Meusel, his teammate with the Phillies and Giants, lived in

California, and Casey got to know Irish's wife, Vandy. The connection was later to prove very important to Casey.

In 1923, Stengel was again employed by McGraw as a part-time platoon player with devasting results for opposing pitchers, as had been the case the previous year. Stengel appeared in seventy-five games for the Giants, fifty-seven in the outfield and eighteen as a pinchhitter. He hit .339 and produced forty-three runs batted in on seventy-four hits, again making another valuable contribution to another Giants pennant. The race had much the same shape as that of 1922, with the primary threats to the favored Giants coming from Cincinnati which finished second and Pittsburgh which came home third. The Giants wound up with a four-and-one-half-game margin and were matched in the World Series against the Yankees for the third straight fall. But this time several things were different. The Yankees were stronger than ever, having demolished the American League, winning the flag by sixteen games over Detroit and sixteen and one half over Cleveland. The new Yankee Stadium was open and the Series would be played there for the first time. And, lastly, the Yankees were to win the Series, but they got a struggle from Casey Stengel before securing their first World Championship.

The opening game of the Series was played in the Bronx and it was deadlocked into the ninth, 4—4, with Bullet Joe Bush toiling for the Yankees. Stengel had singled earlier and had also drawn a walk as the starting center field. Casey had hit only five homers all year for the Giants, but he caught one of Bush's fast balls and smashed it into deep center field in the mammoth ballpark. Bob Meusel, Irish's brother, was the Yankee center field. He was fleet afoot and strong of arm. The ball sailed over his head toward the wall and Stengel set sail around the bases. During the course of the long season, the aging Stengel had suffered a bruised heel and he was wearing a sponge rubber pad in his shoe to cushion the pressure. As he churned around second, the pad came out of his shoe and Stengel thought that his shoe was coming off. But he kept pushing his tiring legs toward third and around the bag. With the relay coming in from the outfield and the crowd of 55,307 in hysterical uproar, Stengel chugged home. As much from exhaustion as anything else, Stengel made a desperate slide

GIANTS TRAINING WITH MEDICINE BALL. CASEY IS ABOUT TO CATCH BALL.

FIRST WORLD SERIES GAME AT YANKEE STADIUM SAW CASEY WIN THE GAME FOR THE GIANTS WITH AN INSIDE THE PARK HOME RUN.

into the plate. But, perhaps fortunately, the throw was a shade off-line and a split-second late, and Yankee catcher Wally Schang was unable to block the plate.

Stengel's Giants mates had swarmed out of the dugout on the first base side, nearly filling the foul ground and were rooting him home as he raced Meusel's arm. When he scored, they mobbed him and convoyed him back to the dugout amidst an assault of slaps and pats of congratulations. The Giants retired the Yanks in the ninth and won the first Series game ever played at Yankee Stadium, 5—4. Stengel was a hero. He was also great copy and was celebrated in newspapers coast-to-coast. The analogy between Stengel and "Casey at the Bat" was too tempting to resist, and he made headlines.

McGraw knew full well that Stengel's days as a Major Leaguer were numbered, but his judgment of Stengel, the clown, as a clutch ballplayer was fully vindicated.

The hero of game one sat on the bench until the ninth inning of game two when he became defensive replacement in the 4—2 Yankee win, which evened the Series. Back at Yankee Stadium, the lure of the headlines was too strong for Stengel in the third game, and he once again became a hero. With Bush again on the mound, Casey, who was zero-for-two at this point, ripped a line drive into the right-field stands, sending the crowd of over 62,000 into tumultuous roaring for the second time in three days. The homer proved to be the only run of the game and the Giants won, 1—0. Back at the Polo Grounds, the Yankees captured game four, 8—4, but Stengel was two-for-two, scoring once and driving in a run. Still, Cunningham was used by McGraw as a pinchhitter for Stengel in the ninth. He struck out.

Addressing a huge audience of newspapermen after his third game, Stengel said, "That makes it Stengel two, the Yankees one. What happened to the rest of the Giants?"

Baseball fans everywhere were asking that question after the fifth game at Yankee Stadium when the Yankees again won, 8—1, with Stengel driving home the only Giants run. The Yanks closed it out the next day at the Polo Grounds, 6—4, with Stengel appearing as a pinchhitter against "Sad" Sam Jones and fouling out in the eighth. He would never appear in another Series as a player, but the

World Series had not seen the last of Casey Stengel by a long shot. Overall, Casey hit .417 in the Series and, for his career, was a .394 hitter in three Series, one for Brooklyn and two for the Giants.

Meanwhile, back in Glendale, California, a young lady named Edna Lawson was following Stengel's exploits against the Yankees with more than casual interest.

During the summer of 1923, Miss Lawson had been planning to vacation in Portland, Oregon. Instead, her friend Vandy Meusel, persuaded her to accompany her to New York since Van's husband played for the Giants and had access to theater tickets and, of course, baseball passes and other items. After a side trip to Atlantic City in mid-July, Mrs. Meusel and Edna Lawson headed back to New York with a number of the baseball wives who had also been in Atlantic City.

Speaking of the Atlantic City interlude later, Edna said, "Some of the other baseball wives were there, and most of the conversation was that they wanted me to meet a very eligible bachelor on the club named Casey Stengel, who was a lot of fun and a very good dancer and a big spender. Of course, all these qualifications were along the line that any girl would be seeking who was taking a vacation. We went to New York when the team came back [from a road trip] and at the ballpark the girls pointed out Casey. Afterward we waited for the men to get dressed. And, finally, along came Casey Stengel."

However, the future Mrs. Casey Stengel had a date that night "with a doctor from Brooklyn" and, somewhat pleased and a trifle surprised, she had to beg off until the next evening when Mr. Stengel asked for the pleasure of her company at dinner that night.

During the course of the next week, Stengel and Miss Lawson were constantly together after the Giants games, but they were seldom alone. They traveled in the company of the other players and their wives. The pair met again in Chicago while Edna was visiting some friends and Casey proposed. She did not accept, but she agreed to continue corresponding.

A few weeks after the end of the World Series, John McGraw departed New York for a European vacation with his wife. However, before he left, he concluded a deal that

was met with varying reactions by those involved. The
Boston Braves wanted the Giants' veteran shortstop, Dave
Bancroft, to manage their club. McGraw decided to accom-
modate them so as not to obstruct Bancroft's chances at being a Major League manager. McGraw obtained outfielder
Bill Southworth, later a distinguished big league manager
himself, and pitcher Joe Oeschger, one of the pitchers in
the longest baseball game ever played in the majors (a
twenty-six-inning, 1−1 tie between Boston and Brooklyn
in 1920). To complete the package, McGraw sent Bancroft,
Billy Cunningham, and Stengel to Boston. Bancroft was
pleased at having a managerial opportunity, Cunningham
was stoic, and Stengel was mad. "I suppose," he said, "if
I'd have hit three homers in the Series this year, they'd
have sent me to the Three-I League [a midwest Minor
League]."

Boston's record for continuously failing to be a contending team was almost notorious and there were places
Stengel had hoped to be spending his final seasons in
baseball as an active player besides the Braves' field. But
playing for Bancroft, a friend from the Giants, he thought
might have its positive side and, in any case, it was better
than not having a job at all.

Stengel spent a large portion of his off-season time and
a considerable amount of his World Series check in the
pleasant pursuit of Edna Lawson, who still remained
somewhat aloof in her father's real estate office in Glendale.

In time, the 1924 season opened and Stengel found
himself back in the unaccustomed position of being a
regular outfielder once more. Under Bancroft, the Braves
were just as terrible as they had been under Fred Mitchell
the year before, finishing dead last with a 53−100 record.
But Stengel played in 131 games, the most he had appeared
in since 1917 at Brooklyn—126 of them as an outfielder,
and the balance as a pinchhitter. He hit a creditable .280
and played more games than any other outfielder on the
club.

It was during a western road trip that Stengel finally
gained the consent of Miss Lawson to marry him. At the
end of a series against the Cardinals in St. Louis, Stengel
crossed the Mississippi River to Belleville, Illinois, where

STENGEL IN THE OUTFIELD FOR THE GIANTS IN 1922.

Edna's brother Larry lived. The ceremony was performed August 18, 1924, at the home of the Catholic Bishop there. At the end of that season, the Stengels went on a tour to Europe with the Giants and the Chicago White Sox, after which they stopped in Kansas City to see Casey's parents, and then journeyed on to Glendale, where they resided until Stengel's death, in a home that was a wedding gift from Edna's father.

Always the clown, after the wedding, Stengel told reporters traveling with the Braves, "If you're going to print anything about us, you can say it was the best catch I ever made in my career."

The European adventure proved to be a great deal of fun for the newlyweds and also a chance to do a favor for John McGraw who was managing what was really a collection of National Leaguers against the Chicago aggregation that included men from other American League clubs.

Stengel's penchant for producing when the spotlight was on brightly manifested itself in England. A game was played in Yorkshire with King George V and his son, the future George VI, in attendance. Becoming aware of the royal presence, Stengel whacked a long home run to contribute to the National Leaguers' victory. Somewhat to his annoyance, George Bernard Shaw, who covered the game for the London *Evening Star*, was singularly unimpressed by Stengel's blast.

Another highlight of the lengthy tour occurred when the teams reached Manila in the Philippines. Stengel, among others, was called upon to deliver a speech. Having watched several preceding speakers struggle to impress the huge throng assembled, Stengel decided to make it as easy as possible to make himself clear. He strode to the front of the platform and launched into a diatribe accompanied by all manner of animated gestures, stomping, and waving of arms. He carried on in this fashion for several minutes without ever uttering a single word. His speech was unspoken. When he completed it and sat down, he received by far the largest ovation of the day. Stengel had done McGraw another favor.

Actually, he was to do his old mentor a more meaningful turn during the season. Brooklyn was closing in on the Giants in the final week of the season when the lowly

Braves knocked them out in a clutch game. Stengel's bases-loaded single in the tenth inning produced the winning runs for the Braves. The Giants finished one and one-half games in front of the hard-charging Dodgers.

The following season was Stengel's first as a married man and his last as a big league player.

In 1925, Bancroft was determined to rebuild the Braves and he started in the outfield. The three outfielders, Stengel, Cunningham, and Frank Wilson, who had played the most games the previous year, were all replaced. Wilson and Cunningham were gone and Stengel rode the bench. He played only one game in the outfield early in the season and appeared in eleven other contests as a pinchhitter. But Bancroft sought to help his old friend, and the club president called Stengel into his offices in mid-May to inform him that the Braves had just purchased the last-place club in the Eastern League, Worcester, as a farm team. He asked Stengel to go there to run the operation from top to bottom.

Thus, on May 22, 1925, Casey Stengel became the president, general manager, and playing field manager of the Worcester club. When he arrived on the scene, the club was 10 – 17 and was, indeed, last in the eight-team circuit. Stengel's two best players were Ed Eayrs, a one-time Braves pitcher who had a brief tryout as an outfielder at Brooklyn, and Stengel himself. Eayrs finished the year hitting .357 to lead the league and Stengel batted .320, slamming ten homers. He whipped the team into shape and drove them home fourth by winning seventy of the last 125 games to finish 80 – 72 overall.

With his first season as a manager under his belt, Stengel was to get a rather surprising boost from an unexpected quarter. Two Toledo, Ohio, lawyers decided that the real estate around the local ballpark, Swayne Field, was a worthwhile investment. They sought to buy it and discovered that it was owned by the New York Giants. Since the Toledo club was a chronic money-loser, the cagey McGraw told the two attorneys that he would not sell them the park unless they bought the team, too.

The attorneys, Oscar Smith and John McMahon, protested to McGraw that they knew absolutely nothing about running or managing a baseball team. But they were interested in Swayne Field, or more specifically, the area around it, and they might entertain the idea of buying the team if McGraw would give them somebody to run the team. McGraw said that he could not provide anyone from the Giants organization, but added, "I can recommend the best man, I think, for you in the operation of the ball club, who can handle and develop players, manage the club properly, and in addition has business ability."

Casey Stengel was McGraw's recommendation.

Smith and McMahon then set out to contact Stengel. They offered him $10,000 a year and an unlimited expense account with which to entertain Major League scouts. In those days, one of the largest sources of revenue for Minor League teams was the sale of players to big league clubs. Virtually all of the Minor League teams were independently owned, and the higher classification clubs bought players from the lower classification ones and then the Triple-A teams sold them to the Majors. Toledo was a member of the American Association, then, as now, a Triple-A League.

However, there was a major stumbling block in the way of Stengel taking this generous and tempting offer. He was already employed by the Boston Braves for the Worcester club. Stengel applied to Judge Fuchs for his release, but the Boston president declined, preferring, if possible, to keep Stengel at Worcester. But Casey took on this challenge. Since he held all of the principal positions at Worcester, he set about relieving himself of them in rapid-fire order.

One of the reasons Stengel was anxious to leave Worcester was the overall condition of the Boston Braves. Although generally not a contending club, Bancroft's shuffling had improved their standing from eighth in 1924 to fifth in 1925, with several young players filling key positions. Stengel had thought the Worcester job might open up the possibility of returning to Boston as the Braves' manager if the team did not improve. When Bancroft improved the club substantially, Casey felt that the way might be blocked by his old friend and he was stingy and clearly would not pay a minor league manager, club president, or anybody else a substantial salary if they could avoid it.

Stengel had no way of knowing that Bancroft would slip back into seventh place in 1926 and, after another

STENGEL RECEIVES SERIES RING FROM JUDGE LANDIS IN 1923.

seventh-place finish in 1927, would be dismissed in favor of Jack Slattery in 1928 who, in turn, would be replaced by playing manager Rogers Hornsby. Hornsby was fired after the 1928 season, despite winning the batting title, and by 1929, Judge Fuchs himself was managing the team in desperation. The Braves finished seventh again in 1928 and dead last in 1929.

In any case, Stengel wanted to get out of the Boston organization after his 1925 experiences. Thus, as general manager, he released the playing manager Casey Stengel. As president, he fired the general manager, Stengel, and then resigned as president. Now considering himself a free agent, he accepted the Toledo position as playing manager and general manager.

The echoes of these moves were heard in the office of Baseball Commissioner Landis who was none too pleased with Stengel's cute little machinations.

Landis threatened to rule Stengel's actions at Worcester null and void. Judge Fuchs finally wrote to Landis, "If that's the way Stengel wants it, let him go. We're better off without him."

But, for many years thereafter, there was a strong, though unconfirmed, rumor in the Major Leagues that Landis would never let Stengel return to the big leagues. When he had an opportunity to manage at Brooklyn, the directors of the Dodgers took precautions by clearing the matter with Landis before firmly offering the post to Casey.

But there was one man in the Eastern League who was greatly impressed by Stengel as a manager and an executive, and was even somewhat amused by the escape hatch Stengel so cleverly utilized to make good his getaway from Worcester. That man was George Weiss, a Yale graduate who was then running the New Haven club in the Eastern League. It was, of course, the same Weiss who was years later to hand Stengel his most magnificent opportunity at a point when almost every other sound baseball man felt that Casey Stengel had reached the end of the road. Stengel always stoutly maintained that, despite the positive reports from the Yankee West Coast scouts, Bill Essick and Joe Devine, and his own friendship with Del Webb, Weiss was mostly responsible for Stengel's chance to manage the Yankees in 1949.

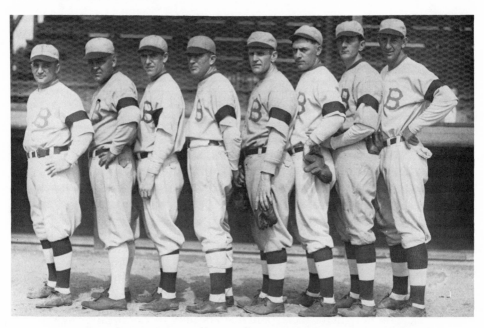

1924 BOSTON BRAVES (L TO R) ARE: R.G. EMMERICH, R. NIXON, WILLIAM J. MCGUIRE, WILLIAM G. CUNNINGHAM, STENGEL, EDWIN SPERBER, WALTER E. CRUISE AND WILLIAM M. BOGWEIL.

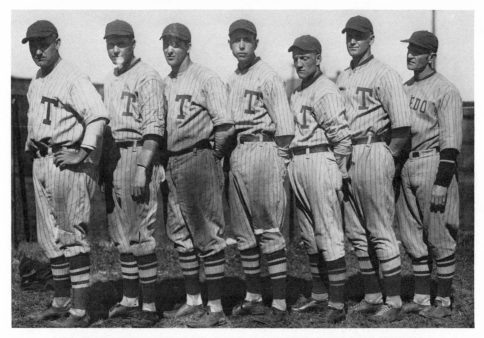

STENGEL'S FIRST TEAM, (L TO R) ARE: HANK MYERS, JIM TANNERY, RIP KOHLER, HARRY MCGUIRE, TOMMY LONG, FRED JOHNSON AND STENGEL OF TOLEDO, 1926.

At Toledo, Stengel inherited a situation that was, at best, in a state of flux. The sale of the club itself cut the connection with the New York Giants and left the press and fans wondering what was going to transpire at Swayne Field in 1926. Whatever they may have imagined, Casey Stengel undoubtedly defied their imagination.

The Toledo situation had several appeals for Stengel. He was able, in fact, to function completely unfettered by any ties to a Major League organization. He would be able to create and market talent totally unencumbered by anybody over him. Further, the owners were ready to acknowledge that they lacked any expertise in baseball whatsoever and were more than willing to take Casey's advice on any phase of the operation. Then, there was the money, which was something above average for a Minor League club in the 1920s and was on a par with what many Major League managers were earning. Normally, Minor League managers were paid a small percentage on the sales they might make of players to higher-level clubs. Stengel did not accept such percentages at Toledo but was, because of his successful performance, very highly rewarded by Smith and McMahon, for whom he made a considerable amount of money.

Another activity Stengel engaged in at Toledo was the utilization of the platoon system to which he himself had been subjected by McGraw while with the Giants. Stengel came to believe that if he had remained with the Giants on McGraw's regimen, it might well have prolonged his career in the Major Leagues by several years, although he disliked the system intensely while he was a part of it. This system became a part of Stengel's philosophy, which he carried with him throughout his long career as a manager, though he did not become commonly known in baseball for his platooning until he turned out the championship team in Oakland years later. The Oakland situation was somewhat similar to that in Toledo in that the team was a combination of veterans and youngsters. Stengel always felt that in any situation of that type platooning was very effective.

Casey's departure from the Eastern League to the American Association was a step up in several ways and, among other things, it saved the New Haven general manager many hours of sleep. Weiss and Stengel would

make a point of comparing notes on baseball, despite the
fact that they were rivals, and Weiss once remarked, "I
guess I have stayed up later and talked longer—or, rather,
listened longer—with Casey than with anybody else in
baseball."

Weiss found those impressions very valuable and
Stengel was to find Weiss very valuable in later years. But
Toledo was another opportunity for Stengel to learn and
create more impressions.

CHAPTER 4

Maverick Manager

Once in Toledo Stengel immediately set to work to make something out of the club, replacing whatever had been removed when the Giants sold it. He was able to round up enough personnel to get things going for the 1926 season, but he had forewarned the new owners not to expect too much from the makeshift collection of hopefuls and has-beens.

Actually, the club did better than anyone, including Casey, had a right to expect under the circumstances, finishing fourth, ten games over .500.

Somewhat to their surprise, the newlywed Stengels found Toledo very much to their liking. They made many lifelong friends and spent many very happy years there. But the happiest year of all was 1927.

America was booming—radio was the latest rage, talking pictures about to be born, bathtub gin was everybody's favorite drink—and the Toledo Mudhens won the American Association pennant. It was, in a very true sense, the Golden Age of sport and, for Stengel, it was a wonderful time to have a winner. Fans flocked to Swayne Field in record numbers. The season attendance of 324,000-plus was almost equal to some of the National League clubs Stengel would manage a decade later.

The owners made more money than they had ever imagined could be realized from a part-time venture like a baseball club. They decided to spend much of the profits in renovating the ballpark.

Toledo became the absolute scourge of the American Association that season. Stengel began the season juggling and maneuvering as usual, but as the campaign wore on and he sensed that the team could win a pennant, he drove hard his combination of youth and age. At the finish, the club was 101−67. The next Stengel club to break the 100-win standard was nearly twenty years later at Oakland in 1946.

Stengel, meanwhile, became a master at the sale of talent to the majors and increased the club's profits even more with shrewd deals. He wound up selling some players two or three times to different teams, getting them back in the interim for a small price or free. He also became a master at holding out a hot hitter against a tough pitcher to save a few points on his batting average or to avoid having him be seen in a bad light by a big league scout.

Among those who played for Stengel at Toledo and were sold by him to big league clubs were Fred Maquire and Woody English, who went to the Cubs, and Roy Parmalee, whom he sold to McGraw for the Giants. One of the men who Casey did the most business with was Bevo LeBourveau. LeBourveau was a highly-skilled man who was, to say the least, inconsistent. But Stengel sold him once to McGraw, once to Connie Mack, and once to Branch Rickey, and each time managed to get him back. Stengel was probably the only Minor League manager in baseball history who got an edge on three of the game's brightest minds, all with the same player.

Though Casey and Edna were happy at Toledo and the owners of the club were happy with the Stengels, the American Association wasn't always happy with Casey. On more than one occasion Stengel got himself tangeled up in little disciplinary problems which resulted in fines from the league office at Columbus.

Always inclined to stand up for what he thought were his rights, Stengel got involved in a few riotous incidents with the Mudhens. But, after 1927, they represented the highlights of the Toledo action. The steady sales of top prospects to the majors caused the Toledo club to decline somewhat in the standings. In his last four years there, Stengel's clubs won 302 games and lost 354, finishing over .500 only once. His 1928 club slipped from its pennant-winning pace of the year before to a sixth place finish and a 79-88 record.

The 1929 Toledo club was a dismal 67-100 and finished last in the eight-team circuit. In the fall of 1929, of course, the Great Crash hit the stock markets and started the slide into the Depression. Fortunately, the next season the Mudhens improved to third place with an 88-66 log, helping keep the club solvent. But the bottom really fell out in 1931. The team staggered through the season with 68 wins and 100 losses, ending up seventh.

**STENGEL, MANAGER OF TOLEDO MUDHENS IN 1926 MEETS WITH
GIANTS' MANAGER JOHN McGRAW, BEFORE EXHIBITION GAME.**

But the general economic conditions were even worse and, more than any other factor, they spelled the end of Stengel's time in Toledo.

"Five of the six banks in which we kept our money closed in 1931," Stengel said later. Worse, the Major League clubs were unwilling or unable to pay large sums for promising prospects. Unemployment reduced attendance sharply, people were standing in bread lines instead of ticket lines.

The Toledo team was taken over from Smith and McMahon at the end of 1931 by the Cleveland Indians. Cleveland, seeking to employ its own loyal personnel, was little interested in keeping Casey at work on the shores of Lake Erie. So, once again, Stengel was out of work.

He was rescued by an old friend and former teammate at Pittsburgh, Max Carey, who was then manager of the Dodgers at Brooklyn. Even in the days when big league clubs commonly only carried two coaches and a manager, Carey was anxious to have Stengel on his staff and offered Casey a job as a coach for the Dodgers. With the Depression now in its midst, Stengel readily accepted.

The Brooklyn situation was a curious one in that the long-time manager of the Dodgers, Wilbert Robinson, had finally been dismissed because of a confrontation with the front office rather than because of any of the fabled misdeeds of the so-called Daffy Dodgers. Babe Herman getting hit on the head with a fly ball (a story Herman always denied) had little, if anything, to do with Uncle Robbie's undoing at Ebbets Field. But his confrontation with Steve McKeever, one of the principal owners, had everything to do with it.

Robinson was undoubtedly the perfect leader for the Flatbush flock. He was keenly aware of the temperament of the Brooklyn fans and was an astute manager. He was the leader of the flock from 1914 to 1931, and during those years he conducted the club to pennants in 1916 and 1920. When his material was decent, the club was competitive, and Robbie made a fight of it even when the team was terrible. He also had the personality to absorb the vagaries that his players sometimes subjected Brooklyn managers to by their malfeasance on the diamond.

Robbie was very close to Charlie Ebbets. After Eb-

bets' death in 1925, internal disputes began to break out in
the front office (located at 215 Montague Street, Brooklyn)
with the directors feuding openely with one another, often
conducting the business of the club through the press in the
days when there were still several daily papers just in
Brooklyn.

The McKeever heirs and the Ebbets heirs each owned
half of the team, and the club began to get heavily indebted
to the Brooklyn Trust Company because of the steady bor-
rowing it did to meet its obligations. Steve McKeever and
his brother, Ed, were the contractors who built Ebbets
Field and acquired half of the stock in the club when Ebbets was unable to pay off the construction costs.

Steve McKeever had originally been a plumber;
Gilleadeau, a haberdasher; Tom York an attorney who
represented the Ebbets' interests; and Robinson a player
for the old Orioles, a teammate of John McGraw's and a
butcher in Baltimore during the off-season.

Steve McKeever finally fired Robinson, over the ob-
jections of Joe Gilleadeau, an Ebbets representative. During the days when the team was something of a laughing
stock. Robinson was once quoted as saying, "What do you
expect of a ball club with a board of directors like ours; a
plumber, a hatter, a lawyer, and a butcher? We're lucky to
keep out of an asylum."

Into this melange, after Robinson was canned, came
Max Carey. Robbie had managed the Dodgers into fourth-
place finishes in each of his last two seasons, and Carey improved it to third in 1932, his first year. But in 1933, the
team dropped to a dismal sixth, seventeen games behind
fifth-place St. Louis and twenty games under .500. Carey
was now on his way out, even though he had a year to go on
his contract.

Observing all of this from afar was the former Dodger,
Casey Stengel, who had many friends in the Brooklyn organization. His theory was that the Dodger club was getting
old and was in need of rebuilding. "I was surprised," he
said, "people didn't realize he [Carey] had a club getting
near the end of its age. But in February of 1934, they called
me to New York City."

After having served for two years as a coach under
Max Carey, Stengel was about to be offered his old friend's

job as manager. It was his first big league managing opportunity, but he was not entirely thrilled about the circumstances. He was greatly concerned about Carey and after the job was formally offered to him, he insisted on calling Max at his Florida home to discuss the matter.

"They told me Carey was out and offered me the managing job. I said, 'Well, I understand Carey's got another year on his contract.' They looked at me and said, 'That's what he has. Max Carey has a contract for another year.' "

But Stengel was unable to determine from his employers whether or not Carey was going to be paid for that remaining year on his contract. Even after calling Carey, he was not sure. But Max told him that, unhappy as he was about what had happened, it had nothing to do with Stengel and he should take the job. Actually Carey had been called from Brooklyn just a few moments before Stengel arrived in the executive offices and was told then for the first time that he had been fired.

Stengel renewed his conversation with the Brooklyn directors by asking, "Well, for goodness sakes, does he get his money or doesn't he?"

McKeever replied, "That's not for you to worry about. The information we'll give you is that if you don't take this job, there are fifty others who will." He was, of course, right, and Stengel accepted the job. Carey was paid for the final year of his contract, as is customary, although Stengel was not really sure. He was offered a one-year contract and became the Dodger field boss for 1934.

He inherited a team that was, in fact, closing in on the end of its collective life. But Stengel's adventures in Brooklyn were to increase and reinforce his reputation as a clown and, more importantly, provide him with an ever-increasing storehouse of knowledge.

Shortly before Stengel's appointment as manager of the Dodgers, Giants manager Bill Terry, as manager of the defending league champions was asked to give a forecast for 1934. After discussions on virtually every other team in the National League, Terry was asked to comment on the Dodgers. He said, "Oh, is Brooklyn still in the league?"

The 1934 season was hardly a banner season at Ebbets Field. Stengel's club was basically Sam Leslie at first, Tony

STENGEL AS DODGER MANAGER, 1934.

Cuccinello at second, Lonney Frey at short, Joe Stripp at third, Al Lopez catching, and Buzz Doyle, Len Koenecke, and Danny Taylor in the outfield. Frey, at twenty-three, was the youngest man in the lineup, having replaced the veteran Glenn Wright at short. Every other regular was over twenty-five although Stengel had replaced the aging Johnny Frederick and Hack Wilson in the outfield.

It was during the 1934 season that one of the funniest incidents of the Stengel regime there occurred. The Dodgers were playing the Phillies early in the year at Baker Bowl when Stengel went out to the mound for about the fifth time to remove his pitcher, Walter Beck. Beck was a twenty-nine-year-old right-hander with a temper. Several times during the game he had talked Stengel out of removing him. This time, Casey was adamant. "Give me the ball, Walter," he said sternly. His pitcher then wheeled in anger and fired the ball into right field. It sailed against the sheet-metal fence at Baker Bowl with a resounding "boom" and caromed back into right field. Wilson, evidently daydreaming, scrambled after it and fired a perfect throw to second.

Wilson, holder of the National League records for homers (fifty six) and runs batted in (190) in a season while with the Cubs in 1930, was for years afterward kidded about chasing that thrown ball.

Stengel, returning to the dugout told Beck, "You're right about one thing, Walter. There's nothing wrong with your arm." But there might have been something wrong with Beck's temper. Later, Casey warned him about kicking water buckets and told him not to repeat the angry outburst. When Beck demanded to know why Stengel objected to his kicking water buckets after being shelled out of a game, Casey replied, "You might break your foot and I wouldn't be able to trade or sell you."

Beck, in later years a pitching coach in the American League, was 2−6 that year and was released back to the minors. But he took with him a nickname earned for his tantrums—"Boom-Boom."

As it turned out, the 1934 season was saved in the last two days. Brooklyn fans, embittered by the very existence of the New York Giants, were absolutely incensed by Terry's cheerful, but sarcastic, comment of the previous fall. While the Dodgers wallowed along in the second division most of the season, the Giants were in first place for 127 days during the race, despite a pell-mell battle with the Cardinals and their ace pitching brothers, Dizzy and Daffy Dean.

On September 28, Dizzy Dean shut out Cincinnati, 4−0, and left the Giants and Cardinals dead even at 93−58, tied for first with two days to go in the season.

The Giants were home at the Polo Grounds against Stengel's Dodgers, while the Cardinals were continuing their series with Cincinnati. Since both Cincinnati and Brooklyn were well down in the standings, it was thought necessary that the Giants beat the Dodgers twice because it was reasonable to assume St. Louis would be able to get two from the Reds. This situation, of course, would have forced the first pennant playoff in National League history. The Giants were slight favorites because of their presence in first place virtually all year. St. Louis had been the league leader (or shared in the lead) for only nine days, from May 28 to June 5.

Stengel was inclined to do anything he could to prevent the Giants from winning the pennant at his expense. The Dodger pitching staff contained one genuine Major League star. Van Lingle Mungo, a sometimes moody twenty three-year-old right-hander had won seventeen games with the sixth-place Dodgers when the teams took the field at the Polo Grounds on September 29. He had also lost sixteen games, but that was more of a function of the ineptness of the club than his inability to pitch. Of the 208 games won by Brooklyn during Stengel's three seasons as their manager, exactly one-quarter, or fifty two games, were won by Van Lingle Mungo.

Mungo won his eighteenth game of the season that afternoon, turning back the Giants with a superb 5−1 effort. Since St. Louis won, 6−1, behind Daffy Dean, the Cardinals moved into first place by a game. On the final day of the season, the Giants needed desperately to win to force a tie. Dizzy Dean, pitching with one day's rest, shutout Cincinnati, 9−0, but Stengel's boys were equal to the task and thumped the Giants for the second straight day, 8−5.

As a result of the Dodgers' doings, the Cardinals won the pennant by two full games. Brooklyn was overwhelmed by rejoicing. Stengel himself was somewhat overwhelmed, too. The big crowd at the Polo Grounds included thousands of Flatbush faithfuls who had trekked over to New York to root the Dodgers home. After the game, Stengel took the subway back toward his Brooklyn home. Hundreds of Dodgers fans had waited on Eighth Avenue behind the Polo Grounds clubhouse for their heroes, and Stengel was nearly mobbed by them. The subway train was converted into a rolling victory celebration, and Stengel later reflected that the ride was one of the most interesting, but physically exhausting, of his life.

Unfortunately, the double defeat of the Giants in 1934 was the highlight of Stengel's years at Brooklyn. Oddly, he was often done in by his own wisdom and the almost-good-enough quality of his team. Mungo aside, pitching was the downfall of the Dodgers. Among those who hurled for the Stengel Dodgers were Tom Zachary, forty at the time, and George Earnshaw, thirty-six. Building a pitching staff around such aged men, wily and crafty though they were, was almost impossible.

Bouyed by their garrison finish against New York, the 1934 Dodgers finished with a 71−81 record in sixth place.

In 1935, things were pretty much the same, producing a 70−83 record and a fifth-place finish.

But the most enduring part of the Stengel years at Ebbets Field came in the form of the fascinating and hilarious stories Casey accumulated.

One of his favorite topics for stories for years was Frenchy Bordagaray. Frenchy was an outfielder and sometimes second baseman who was a regular on Stengel's last two Dodgers clubs in 1935 and 1936. He was a .282 hitter in 1935 and a .315 batsman in 1936, leading the club in stolen bases both years. Bordagaray was clearly not without talent, but as one writer once pointed out, "Frenchy's speed might have really helped the Dodgers if he had run in the right direction."

Bordagaray was prone to daydream on the field and on the bases. One day in 1935, Stengel was holding down his accustomed post in the third base coaches' box with Bordagaray on second. Billy Jurges was playing shortstop for the Cubs and he slipped in behind Bordagaray with the ball. When Jurges tagged him, the umpire called Frenchy out and Stengel shot out of the coaches' box toward the arbiter in full sail. The crowd responded warmly since Bordagaray was standing on the bag at second when the out call was made and the prospect of a lively argument started and saved an otherwise dismal afternoon for the Dodger fans.

On his way across the infield, Stengel noticed that Bordagaray was quietly trotting off to the dugout without raising a single note of protest over the obviously erroneous call. Stengel stopped Bordagaray and inquired as to why he was not arguing the call.

"You were safe weren't you?" Stengel asked Frenchy, as the umpire headed toward left field.

"Nope," Frenchy responded, "I was out."

Stengel was now stuck with the prospect of arguing with an umpire when his own player had conceded that the call was correct. He headed out into the outfield and ran through the motions of a brief dispute, throwing his hat down on the outfield grass and waving his arms briefly to give the bleacherites their money's worth. He then headed back to the bench and attacked Bordagaray.

"I saw your foot on the bag," Stengel yelled. "How could Jurges tag you out?"

"It was this way, Case," Frenchy replied. "I'm standing near second base doing this tap dance. I guess he just tagged me in between taps."

Perhaps the classic Bordagaray story in the Stengel repetoire concerned a fine Casey once leveled on his prize banana. Stengel described the incident thusly: "One day we were playing the Giants at the Polo Grounds and Frenchy hit a double. He wanted to steal third, but I wouldn't let him. But when the next batter singled to left, I waved Frenchy home. He was fast then and could outrun a horse. Joe Moore fielded the ball and you know what an arm Joe had. He whipped it in with Gus Mancuso [the Giants' catcher] standing nonchalantly at the plate as though he were waiting for a street car. Suddenly he reached out, grabbed the ball and tagged Frenchy, who had been conned into neglecting to slide, for an out which cost us a run."

After the game, Stengel told Bordagaray in the

clubhouse that the base-running mistake would cost him
$25. Bordagaray said, "That was a dumb one, Case, better
make it $50."

Amid uproarious laughter from the other Dodgers,
Stengel immediately agreed and fined Bordagaray $50.
Years later, Stengel was hospitalized in Boston after being
struck by a car and Bordagaray came to visit. "How about
paying me back the $50 you owe me from that fine?" the
visitor asked the patient.

"My uncle has the fifty," Stengel said.

"Which uncle?" Bordagaray questioned.

"Uncle Sam," replied Stengel, and Bordagaray never
got the money back. On the other hand, the fans came to
know of the fine and the reason for it. During the next
season, Bordagaray would always slide into home plate,
whether or not there was a play being made on him by the
other team. The fans at Ebbets Field always responded
with ardent applause to the sight of Bordagaray diving into
home while the opposing outfielders were still chasing a
long drive.

Stengel should have known he had an extraordinary
character on his hands when Bordagaray reported to spring
training sporting a mustache. Frenchy had seen pictures of
pre-1900 ballplayers and sought to emulate them. Stengel
finally made him shave it off. When Frenchy demanded to
know why he had to shave it, Stengel told him, "It's affect-
ing your fielding. It makes you top-heavy."

The unevenness of Bordagaray's performances was a
total frustration to Stengel. Casey was fond of telling a
story about a game the Dodgers played at Forbes Field in
Pittsburgh.

The Dodgers had a one-run lead in the eighth when
Bordagaray committed an error which permitted the Pirates
to score a run to tie the game. Then, in the ninth, he
cracked a long triple and ultimately scored the go-ahead run
with a fast break from third on an infield out.

As the fortunes of baseball would have it, Frenchy
made two outstanding catches of Pittsburgh drives in the
last of the ninth to bring the Dodgers within a out of winning.

"So somebody lifts an easy fly to him," Stengel said
later. "I breath a deep sigh of relief, but suddenly my blood

PITCHER VAN LINGLE MUNGO.

pressure skyrockets. The ball hits Frenchy's glove and bounces straight up in the air. Does that rattle him? Not a bit. He reaches up his bare hand like a trolley conductor grasping for the bell cord and collars the ball for the final out.''

By the time Stengel recovered his composure, Frenchy was already in the locker room shower.

Joining Bordagaray in the outfield antics during 1935 were Taylor, Buzzy Doyle, Koenecke, and Jim Bucher, with Taylor and Doyle the regulars. Bucher also played both second and third and hit .302 for the year, one of three regulars batting over .300. The others were first baseman Sam Leslie (.308) and third baseman Joe Stripp (.306). But the heaviest hitter on the club was pudgy reserve catcher Babe Phelps who posted a .364 average in forty-seven games and had a .579 slugging percentage.

But the bottom really fell out for Stengel and the Dodgers in 1936. The continuing wrangling among the members of the board of directors virtually handcuffed the manager.

"I wasn't even allowed to claim a man at the waiver price," Stengel said later. The waiver price in 1936 was $6,000.

The early-season attendance was fairly strong since the team had advanced from sixth to fifth place the year before, and Brooklynites were hopeful that the upward trend was going to continue.

But decisions in the front office were to affect this movement as much as anything else. Off-season deals sent away Sam Leslie to the Giants and the two best defensive men in the Dodger lineup, second baseman Tony Cuccinello and catcher Al Lopez, to the Boston Braves. The hard-hitting Phelps was then advanced to starting catcher, but his defensive inadequacies hardly were compensated for by his bat. The one major plus in the off-season shifting was that the Dodgers acquired a thirty-one-year-old outfielder named Randy Moore. Moore was later to make Stengel a rich man by involving him in Texas oil fields.

In 1936, Leslie hit .295 in 117 games for the Giants, and New York won the pennant by five games over Chicago. Boston, bolstered by the defensive work of Cuccinello and Lopez, moved up from eighth in 1935 (when they won an incredible thirty-eight games) to sixth, nearly doubling their victory total. Stengel's crippled Dodgers, meanwhile, stumbled to seventh with a 67−87 record. That they did as well as they did was undoubtedly a testimony to Casey's efforts. At one point in the season, after the directors had sent Zachary to Philadelphia and Earnshaw to St. Louis, the Dodgers had seven pitchers capable of working.

At this juncture one of the healthy pitchers, young George Jeffcoat, twisted his ankle and went to the sidelines, reducing the staff to six healthy bodies. Stengel was then in the midst of a series with Pittsburgh and was facing the prospect of a series with the powerful St. Louis Cardinals, which opened with a doubleheader.

Stengel decided to hoard his pitchers and sent a right-handed kid named Tom Baker out to face Pittsburgh. The Pirates hit Baker hard and he did not help himself by issuing four bases on balls. So Stengel, reluctantly, brought in Max Butcher in relief and decided that was it for the day; everybody else was to be saved for St. Louis and, besides, the Pirates were leading, 8−2.

But the Dodgers kept pounding the Pirate starter, lefty Ralph Birkofer, finally driving him out and tying the score. Stengel effectively became a victim of his own magic. When the Dodgers rallied to tie the score, he used several pinchhitters in the inning, starting with Phelps who delivered a hit. Jimmy Bucher was used and also produced a hit. As the inning continued, Sid Gautreaux came up and made an out, but kept out of a double play and the inning was still alive. Then Stengel used Randy Moore who joked that he later "hadn't been to bat in three months." This was a slight exaggeration, but Moore was, to say the least, a seldom-used hitter. Moore rammed a double to left, producing the tying runs and forcing Stengel to bring in Ed Brandt in a valiant last-ditch effort to win the game.

Pittsburgh nicked Brandt for a run and won the game in ten innings, 9−8.

The net result of all of the turmoil was that Stengel had used up three of his precious pitchers instead of the one he had hoped for and still wound up with nothing to show for it except another digit in the right-hand column. Had his selection of pinchhitters been less astute and had Brooklyn not tied the game, the result probably would have been the

same, but Stengel would have been better off. The following day his exhausted pitching staff went out for the
doubleheader against the Gashouse Gang Cardinals and still
managed to salvage a split. Ironically, Moore had only
three doubles all season.

Throughout all of the disappointment surrounding the
collapsing Dodgers, Stengel managed to maintain his sense
of humor and shrewdly employed comedy as a public relations gesture to gather favorable space in the press for his
terrible team. The entourage of baseball writers traveling
with the Dodgers was without doubt the best-entertained
group of newspapermen in the entire history of the United
States. Long before his early Yankee years when he in-
troduced Stengelese to the world, Casey was a master
storyteller. He would regale the writers with his Minor
League experiences and, often, tell stories about himself
complete with gestures and pantomine.

One of the oft-repeated Stengel stories concerned his
comment to his faltering team at Toledo in 1930 when he
advised them all to buy Pennsylvania and Baltimore & Ohio
Railroad stock at the end of an unhappy clubhouse meeting.

One of the players asked, "Why, is the stock going
up?"

"It should," Stengel responded, " 'cause I'm shipping
a lot of you guys out on the rails pretty soon."

One of the men to whom this message was addressed
was Jocko Conlon, a veteran Minor League outfielder who
played briefly with the White Sox in the mid-1930s but
gained far more renown as a National League umpire for
two decades.

The Brooklyn clubhouse in 1936 bore an eerie re-
semblance to those Toledo days. During the course of the
mad season, thirty-four men wore the Dodger flannels onto
the field for at least one National League appearance. The
problem, however, had nothing to do with quantity. It was
related much more directly to quality. The Dodgers, on the
whole, were lousy. Some of them, of course, had talent.
One of Stengel's newcomers in 1936 was Buddy Hassett, a
young first baseman who replaced Sam Leslie and hit .310
while appearing in all 156 Dodger games. Hassett remained
at Brooklyn after Stengel departed, until the arrival of
Dolph Camilli, who had a lot more power, and made him

FRENCHY BORDAGARAY.

expendable. Stengel then dealt for him and the two rejoined at Boston.

But even Van Lingle Mungo began to show the strain and suffered a losing (18 − 19) season while toiling in forty five games, thirty-seven of them as a starter. But Mungo skipped the club for a few days after Stengel told him if he felt he did not want to play, he should go home. Mungo was depressed and Stengel felt a few days away from the ballpark might help him and also give him an incentive when he realized how much he missed playing baseball. Stengel was right, but the front office was infuriated when they learned that Casey had not only countenanced Mungo's leave, but almost encouraged it. The episode was later held against Stengel when the management decided to make him the scapegoat for the team's poor performance.

The situation had also worsened at Montague Street when Bob Quinn, the skillful and calm business manager, departed after 1935 to become president of the Boston Braves. He and Stengel were later to become reunited when Quinn hired Casey to manage at Boston, but his departure disturbed Stengel and made his situation in Brooklyn even less pleasant.

But Casey hung despite the 67 − 87 record that buried the Dodgers in seventh place, twenty-five games behind the pennant-winning Giants. The fact that New York won the flag made the Brooklyn situation look even worse, if that were possible. But few, if any, of the fans and none of the press blamed Stengel for the situation.

In 1917, when Charles Ebbets traded Stengel to Pittsburgh for Burleigh Grimes and others, it was frankly a good deal for the Dodgers. Grimes, one of the last of the legal spitball pitchers, turned in a strong 19 − 9 season at Brooklyn in 1918 and his 23 − 11 mark in 1920 was largely responsible for the Brooklyn pennant that season.

But twenty years later, it was a question of whether trading Stengel for Grimes again made sense. After the seventh-place finish of 1936, Stengel was let out of his contract at Brooklyn. Having learned from the Max Carey case three years before, Stengel made sure he got his salary for 1937. This meant that Casey was being paid for not managing a club. It also made 1937 the only year from 1910 until 1961 that he was not actively involved on the field with a ballclub, and the only time from 1910 until his death sixty-five years later that he did not hold some position with a team.

Burleigh Grimes had some managerial experience in the minors, but not much, and he was nowhere nearly as successful as Stengel. Nevertheless, he was named to manage the Dodgers for 1937. He brought the club home in sixth place. The following year, Stengel was back in the majors at Boston and finished fifth. Grimes managed the Dodgers to a seventh-place ranking and he, too, was fired.

Finally, the directors decided to attack the problem at its root, in the front office. Larry MacPhail came to Brooklyn from Cincinnati. MacPhail immediately installed lights at Ebbets Field, put the Dodger games on the radio, against the verbal agreement of the three New York clubs, fired Grimes, and hired Leo Durocher as his manager. In 1939, the Dodgers jumped to third and, in 1940, they finished second to the Cincinnati club MacPhail had built before he left Crosley Field. In 1941, Brooklyn won its first pennant since 1920.

Durocher, rightly, receives much of the credit for the dramatic improvement in the Dodgers in the three-year span he served as the club's manager including 1941. But it is highly likely that given the support that Durocher got from MacPhail, Stengel would have done just as well. In 1942, Brooklyn was edged by St. Louis in a furious finish, missing the flag by two games. But by 1944, MacPhail had been in the service for two years and the Dodgers were seventh, forty-two games behind the Cardinals.

At this point, Branch Rickey had become the general manager at Brooklyn and the Dodgers started their resurgence. The great post-war Brooklyn clubs were built by Rickey and won with a variety of managers, none of them named Durocher.

The Dodger pennants were won in the post-World War II era by Burt Shotton (1947 and 1949), Charlie Dressen (1952 and 1953), and Walter Alston (1955 and 1956). All of these men won with essentially the same team, fed by the same farm system and front office operation set up by Mac-Phail and Rickey.

Stengel could have won with that support, too, but not all managers could have won with that talent. Many clubs play better for certain managers and some men can handle certain teams better than others. But without the basic material to work with, no manager can win consistently. The club ownership and management has to supply the manager with some basic tools to achieve his function. The type of material Stengel got in Brooklyn nobody could have won with, but Stengel did better than most with it, and he worked hard to build a future for the Dodgers. He also worked hard to shore up the club's faltering public image and maintain an interest in the club during the depths of the Depression. In his final year, the team fell to seventh, but attendance rose to 489,618, a rise of over 55,000 from the 1934 figure when the team was sixth. Good will with the press and the public was one of Stengel's important legacies at Ebbets Field.

The next team he was to handle in the majors was to suffer from much the same malady. The club was impoverished and the front office handicapped by lack of funds. Stengel did his best to solve that problem, too, by investing his own money in the team. All of these efforts were consistent with Casey's constant dedication to baseball.

PITCHER BURLEIGH GRIMES.

CHAPTER 5

Back to the Minors

The 1937 season was a significant one for Casey Stengel. Now that he was officially out of the game, he was able to use advantageously both the time that year afforded him and the money ($15,000) Brooklyn was paying him for not working. During his years as the Dodgers' manager, Randy Moore, a left-handed outfielder appeared briefly at Brooklyn in 1936. Moore batted .239 with the Dodgers and decided he might do better in the oil business in Texas. In 1937, he approached Stengel and a few other baseball acquaintances (including Al Lopez) to invest in his wells. Stengel took his Dodger money and bought shares in a number of wells. Moore was remarkably successful with his ventures and, as a result, Stengel made a handsome profit. Some of the oil wells were still producing in the 1960s. Combined with his involvement with the Glendale Bank, the oil wells made Stengel a wealthy man.

He had turned down several Minor League opportunities and one Major League coaching offer for 1937, but still retained his interest in returning to baseball.

Bob Quinn, who had left his job as Dodger business manager to become president of the Boston Braves in 1935, offered Stengel the post as not only the manager of the club, but also a partner in its ownership. Quinn had organized the syndicate that purchased the club from C. F. Adams, it previous owner. Adams was financially secure and willing to put money into the club. But he also owned the Suffolk Downs racetrack and Commissioner Landis took a dim view of his being involved with the Braves. He finally tired of being chastized by Landis and sought to unload the club. Quinn gathered a group of his acquaintances from Brooklyn to buy the club, used his baseball influence to get the sale approved, and brought Stengel in as the on-field baseball man. Stengel eventually invested some $50,000 in the team's stock. He was strongly supported by another backer, Max C. Meyer, a Brooklyn jeweler who remained an ardent enthusiast of Stengel's throughout the Boston years.

Throughout the six years the syndicate owned the franchise, Stengel was its manager. The fact that Stengel had a significant interest in the team made his managerial position somewhat more secure than it would have been under normal conditions. Eventually, the club was sold, Stengel's stock was purchased by the new owners, and he resigned as manager. But there was a good deal of interesting adventure before the conclusion of Casey's years at Braves' field.

Stengel and Quinn were handicapped by the same problem that had faced them at Brooklyn—money. Their syndicate of friends who bought the Braves had little capital to invest in acquiring new players of any stature, so Stengel spent most of his efforts in developing new talent.

In 1938, the Braves (who were officially known at the time as the Boston Bees) compiled a 77−75 record and finished fifth, missing the first division by a half dozen games, behind a Cincinnati club managed by Casey's predecessor at Boston, Bill McKechnie. The Reds were to win the pennant in each of the next two seasons. It appeared from the performances of 1938 that Boston might become a contender in the next few years as well. Rookie outfielder Max West was one of the more impressive youngsters in the National League and the pitching, under Stengel's handling, had been more consistent than expected. But, unfortunately for Stengel, the Braves were to decline rather than ascend during the remainder of his years at Boston.

The 1939 season was a grievous disappointment to Stengel. Although West continued to be a mainstay of the club, Boston fell to seventh place with a record of 63−88. Stengel had disposed of some of his players from the first year and was beginning to be criticized for it. One of the men traded (in this case, to the Reds) was Vince DiMaggio, older brother of Joe and Dom. In 1938, DiMaggio played 150 games for the Braves and showed signs of power. But Stengel's judgment was justified in later years when Vince turned out to be the wrong DiMaggio. He drifted off to several National League clubs and his lasting impact in baseball was largely in terms of impressive strikeout totals.

Sometime afterward, Stengel remarked about Vince

DiMaggio, "I helped make him a strikeout king. Now maybe somebody else can develop him into a hitter." Nobody ever did. Wartime personnel shortages helped to prolong Vince's career, but he always lived in the shadow of his two younger brothers.

West, on the other hand, was something of a joy to Stengel. One of Stengel's favorite Max West stories revolved around the fabled double-no-hit effort of Cincinnati's Johnny Vander Meer. On June 11, 1938, the Bees went into Crosley Field and faced the slants of Vander Meer. Stengel's pitcher, Danny MacFayden, fired a tight six-hitter at the Reds. But Vander Meer threw a no-hitter at Boston and won, 3—0. He earned national notoriety four days later with another gem against the Dodgers in the first night game ever played at Ebbets Field.

When Boston next returned to Cincinnati, Vander Meer was scheduled to pitch against them again. A huge crowd packed into Crosley Field expecting Vander Meer to continue his success against Stengel's club. Before the game, Stengel rode out to the park with West and casually inquired as to how the outfielder had hit against Vander Meer. West told him that he usually hit extraordinarily well against the Dutchman. Casey replied, "Well, the park's sold out. They got banners here and there from insurance companies and every kind of companies." The game progressed and Vander Meer had the club beat going into the ninth. So Stengel said to West, "Go up there and hit one out." West did hit one and it won the game. Casey was later to find out that West had got only two hits off Vandy in his life.

But that story was far from finished. The elfish Stengel went on with his tale, "Well, anyway, everybody in Cincinnati was mad the way the game wound up. I got back to the hotel and they were standing around in the lobby in little bunches and they were all beefin'. I'd walk from one bunch to another and I'd say, 'Pardon me, I'm a stranger in town and I had to leave in the seventh. Can you tell me how the ball game came out tonight?' You never heard such squawking and moaning in all your life. I went around like this until they finally recognized me, but I never had such a fine time!"

Stengel always had his eye out for talent at Boston, but

it did not come along that often. The Bees continued to slide and were kept out of the cellar in the eight-team National League of those days only by the fact that the Philadelphia Phillies were downright horrid. Another seventh-place finish was earned in 1940 when the club was 65 – 87. The same place was obtained in 1941 and 1942 with records of 62 – 92 and 59 – 89, the low point of Stengel's managing history in the Major Leagues until the Mets of 1962 and 1963. Stengel's relationship with the press, almost always universally cordial, began to erode through the years of dismal finishes. Some, like Harold Kaese of *The Boston Globe*, stuck by Stengel, saying, "Losing with Stengel was more fun than with a hundred other managers I could name. Unfortunately for the fans, they did not have the benefit of Stengel's company." All of the writers were not so charitable as the years wore on.

In addition to his own ability to perform, Stengel always was on the lookout for players who might be good copy and also give the fans something to talk about.

As a result, Stengel obtained the services of both of the great Waner brothers for brief times. "Little Poison" Lloyd Waner passed through for nineteen games in 1941 and batted .412 as a utilityman before he was sent on to Cincinnati for pitcher Johnny Hutchins on June 12. "Big Poison" Paul Waner was acquired after his release from Brooklyn in May, 1941, and he stayed at the Braves field until 1942. The two, of course, were among the greatest hitters in baseball history and made plenty on ink during their stays with the Braves. Paul hit .279 in 1941 and .258 in 114 games with Boston in 1942 before he was released.

One of Stengel's pet Waner stories was about an incident during spring training before the 1942 season. Stengel was sitting on the bench chatting with Paul Waner and asked him if he could hit one over the whiskey sign in right center. Waner admitted that he could not even see the sign from the bench. Stengel was dismayed and suggested that Waner get glasses. He did and wore the glasses during batting practice a couple of days afterward, and Stengel asked him how the ball looked to him.

"Mighty small," Waner said. "Before it used to look as big as a grapefruit."

"So right then I told him to throw away the glasses and

hit at that big grapefruit, even if it's a blurry grapefruit,'' Stengel related later.

Meanwhile critical comment continued to grow in the Boston papers as the demands of the war gradually stripped the big leagues of most of their talented and younger men. The Braves became a bad team, wallowing in a sea of mediocrity. Other National League teams were also struck by the military need for manpower, but they were still easily better than the Braves.

One of Stengel's heaviest critics was Dave Egan, *"The Colonel,"* whose column was a feature of the *Daily Record* sports pages. Egan once wrote of Casey, "He's a great guy, except for those who work for him. He's a funny guy, too; always funny at somebody else's expense, and that somebody is usually within hearing distance. So he wound up with a sullen ball club and the majority of the players hate him. He ruined some of the young players, yet he always remains funny in his cruel and malicious way." Much of Egan's commentary was, of course, unfair. But things were not exactly a barrel of laughs in the Boston clubhouse. In reality, Stengel had little, if anything, to do with the problems since their roots were actually economic.

Stengel had pieced together a presentable team in his first year at Boston by using all of the tricks he had acquired during his many years in baseball. Despite his lack of hitting ability, Vince DiMaggio was a fine outfielder; the infield was handled by a slick fielder, Tony Cuccinello, the pitching was decent, and the catching was largely in the hands of Al Lopez, who Stengel once said was better at making a low pitch look like a strike than any man he ever saw. Given the prevailing winds off the Charles River which blew in from left field, power hitting was not a major factor in most games at the Braves' field. In the infield, Stengel employed a few tricks that might raise ethical questions, but they helped his defense: sodding the grass with peat moss and soaking down the infield before every game.

But being unable to buy veteran players and to spend money developing new ones, the team slowly collapsed. The Selective Service virtually killed it off.

West, more important to Boston than a man of similar ability would have been to another club, went into the service in 1943. It was the beginning of the end of Stengel's time with the Braves. Struggling to assemble any kind of a Major League team for 1943 was a major trial for Stengel. He lost two of his prime outfielders, West and Nanny Fernandez, before the season opened. What passed as spring training that year was held at the Choate School in Wallingford, Connecticut, and catcher Ernie Lombardi held out during the entire affair, handicapping Stengel's preparation even more. The pitching staff consisted of scraps, much of it past its prime, plus some kids. The vets included Al Javery, Jim Tobin, and Bill Donovan, as well as former Yankee great Lefty Gomez, more than an average wit himself.

One day Stengel, who had spent a lot of time trying to alter Gomez's pitching form, asked "El Goofo" what he thought the major differences were between the National and American leagues.

"The biggest difference," Gomez said, "is that over here in the National League, they don't know that John McGraw has been dead for five years."

Almost immediately, Gomez was no longer a Brave.

Wartime travel restrictions had forced the training at Choate and also eliminated any reasonable kind of exhibition game schedule. But on April 19, two days before the season was to open, the Braves played the Red Sox. After the game, Stengel held a conference with Bob Quinn and the other Braves officials. The meeting lasted long into the night. Stengel headed back to his hotel amidst rain and a wartime security brownout.

In Kenmore Square, he was struck by a car. Stengel never saw the car when it hit him. The fifty-two-year-old manager was sent sprawling. He was taken to St. Elizabeth's Hospital where team physician Dr. Edward J. O'Brien discovered he had suffered fractures of the fibula and tibia bones in his lower right leg. O'Brien was unable to set the bones for a week because of the heavy swelling around the breaks.

Upon learning of the accident, Edna Stengel immediately wired Casey that she was leaving her ailing mother in Glendale to come East to be with him. Stengel wired back, "Don't come unless you can set a broken leg." Edna stayed with her mother.

Stengel immediately asked for a conference with

Quinn and the other officials. True to form, he was more concerned about his team than himself. But Dr. O'Brien ordered the conference postponed until later in the day to give Stengel a chance to get some rest. When the meeting was held, it was determined that Casey would remain manager, but the team would be handled from the bench by coaches George Kelley and Bob Coleman.

Never one to pass by a shot at Stengel, Dave Egan delivered an item in his column in which he cited the cab driver who struck Stengel's "as the man who did the most for baseball in Boston in 1943." By the time Stengel was released from St. Elizabeth's on June 12, the Braves were already mired in the second division and he was only able to bestir them into a sixth-place finish with a 68 – 85 record.

Meanwhile, a disintegration of equal seriousness was developing in the front office. The Braves had become a chronic loser at the box office as well as on the field. In 1938, the Braves drew 341,149 fans. By 1940, the total was off almost 100,000 to 241,616, and it did not improve significantly during the following years. One of the members of the consortium, contractor Lou Perini, had approached Stengel during spring training prior to the 1943 season with a question which Stengel proceeded to answer in his own distinct style. Perini repeated the question, stating that he did not understand the answer. When the same response, with even more irrelevant elaboration, was forthcoming, Perini, singularly unimpressed, walked away.

Perini did not care for Stengel and Casey was not unaware of his feeling and, in fact, to some degree he reciprocated it. As the 1943 season drew toward its unhappy conclusion with Stengel running the club from the dugout on crutches, Perini began negotiating to acquire control of the club for himself and his two brothers. The negotiations continued after the season, and most of the shareholders, including Max Meyer, sold out in mid-January 1944. The Perinis, nicknamed "The Three Steamshovels" in the local press, asked Quinn to remain as president of the club (he was finally replaced by Lou Perini in 1945). Stengel, pointedly, was not asked to remain as field manager, although he had not sold his interest in the club. Aware of the feeling between himself and Perini, Stengel elected to resign rather than force the issue. While in Chicago on business, Stengel wrote a letter to Quinn and on January 27, Quinn announced that Stengel had resigned.

Stengel's letter read, in part; "On my way East I noted in the newspapers that a new group has purchased controlling stock in the Braves baseball club. The papers have been carrying stories whether or not there should be a new manager. Whenever a new group purchases control of a corporation, they have the right to dictate the policy of that corporation. In order that there be no embarrassment for the new group, I hereby tender my resignation."

Further on, the letter contained kind words for his old friend Quinn and also the comment; "No one realized more than you the interest at stake during my tenure as manager and faith I had in the city of Boston. You are familiar with the substantial amount of my personal cash which I invested in the club. You also know that whenever the directors asked for more cash, I put up as much as any other director."

Behind the long letter, intended for publication, lay the deep-seated feelings of sadness that had actually ended Stengel's connection with the Braves. His stock was subsequently acquired by the Perinis, ending his association with Boston.

He was not in desperate need of funds largely thanks to his investment in the Texas oil wells. At this point, Casey decided to retire once more to Glendale.

Charlie Grimm began 1944 as the manager of the Milwaukee farm club in the American Association. In May, Grimm was asked to assume the reigns of the Chicago Cubs. He called Stengel and requested that Stengel, as a favor, take over the Brewers. Not being involved in spring training, though this was only his second time without it since 1910, was disturbing to Stengel. He accepted the Milwaukee job even though it was not the Major Leagues and he really did not plan on spending more than one season in Milwaukee.

As subsequent events were to show, it was well that Casey did not plan on a long tenure in Milwaukee. The Brewers' president at that time was Bill Veeck, later famous as a club owner in the American League at St. Louis, Cleveland, and Chicago. Veeck, at the time, was serving in the military and was ensconced on an atoll in the mid-Pacific. The directors of the Milwaukee club hired Stengel without checking with Veeck. Once he learned of their action, Veeck was furious. That the directors had acted without clearing it with him infuriated him. But he was also incensed because Stengel was the club's choice to succeed Grimm. Veeck felt that Stengel was a second-division manager, whose reputation as a clown was legitimate.

Veeck fired off a letter to the Brewer directors in which he made his feelings abundantly clear. "He is entirely satisfied with a losing ballclub," Veeck wrote, "as long as Stengel and his wit are appreciated. . . . If Stengel has an iron-clad contract and it will be expensive for us to cancel it, I guess that we're stuck with him. But he is not to be rehired next year."

For the wartime conditions then prevailing, Milwaukee had a very sound club. On May 5, Stengel took over the club when it was in first place, and he kept it there through the end of the season on September 10, leading his charges home with the American Association pennant. This marked the first time he had managed a pennant-winning since 1927 at Toledo. Unfortunately, his efforts were lost on Veeck, who was still unconvinced of his ability as a manager.

Milwaukee had won the pennant the year before in the American Association, but had been beaten in the post-season playoffs by third-place Louisville. Exactly the same scenario prevailed in 1944 and with his club eliminated from the playoffs, Stengel was back in Glendale and out of baseball once more, despite his record of 91−49 at the helm of the Brewers.

Then, through the intervention of George Weiss in New York, one of those strange quirks of baseball fate landed Casey Stengel back in the town where he had been fired from his first baseball job as a callow youth in 1910—Kansas City. The Yankees owned the Kansas City Blues of the American Association and had used it as one of their top farm clubs (along with Newark of the International League) for many years. When the manager's job opened for 1945, Weiss contacted Stengel and offered him the highest salary the Yankees had ever paid a manager at Kansas City.

Though Casey and Edna had decided not to take any

more jobs in the minors, Stengel was so flattered by the offer from Weiss and the rather unexpected generosity of his
old friend, he accepted. He accepted knowing that the
Kansas City club was probably the weakest team that had
been fielded there since the Yankees had taken over the
franchise. The Blues had finished last in 1944 and were
stocked with underaged and inexperienced kids blended
with 4-F service rejects. The demands on the Yankee
system to stock the New York club and two triple-A teams
had led to the decision that Kansas City was to get third
choice of talent. Though fully aware of this, Stengel signed
a contract on January 20 and returned to Kansas City.

The Blues lived up to their advance billing. They were
horrid. Kansas City struggled home seventh in the eight-
team American Association although they compiled a record of 65 − 86, which was more than respectable under the
circumstances Stengel faced at Ruppert Stadium. But given
his general feeling about continuing to work and travel in
the minor leagues, Stengel determined not to return to
Kansas City and notified club secretary Roy Hamey of his
intention to resign. He returned to Glendale once more
without a job in baseball.

Another acquaintance, Cookie DiVincenzi, then contacted Stengel about the possibility of his managing
Oakland in the Pacific Coast League in 1946. Since the club
was located in California and played virtually all of its
games in the state, Stengel was interested. Edna pointed
out, "It's close to home and the travel ain't bad."

Stengel went to Oakland to meet the team's owners,
Brick Laws and Joe Blumenfeld. He liked Oakland and was
particularly impressed by the Oakland Bay Bridge. "I like
the idea of bridges," he remarked. "Everywhere I go, they
throw in a bridge as part of the service. Like at Brooklyn.
Besides, every manager wanted to jump off a bridge sooner
or later, and it is very nice for an old man to know he
doesn't have to walk fifty miles to find one."

For whatever reasons, Stengel signed a contract to
manage the Oakland Oaks on October 17, for $12,000. The
money didn't seem like much compared to what Stengel
had made in the majors, or even at Kansas City, but his in-
vestments were paying well and he pointed out that it was

not so bad, "since I made $2,100 for my first year in the majors."

Of course, Stengel did not bother to point out that his first year in the Major Leagues was 1912, thirty-four years earlier.

Stengel later said, "At Oakland I had so many older players I was platooning with, that writers on the Coast commenced calling us 'The Nine Old Men,' like the nickname given to the United States Supreme Court [by President Roosevelt]."

But, with Brick Laws, Stengel was working for one of the most competent executives in the Minor Leagues. Laws knew his baseball, had good business instincts, and worked well with his manager. He worked especially well with Stengel. Many who saw the wireservice announcement that Stengel had accpeted a $12,000 job in the Pacific Coast League had doubtless thought that the Major Leagues had finally seen the end of Casey Stengel. Events were to prove this totally false.

In 1946, Stengel was provided with far better material by Laws than he had lately become accustomed to, but he knew just what to do with it. Stengel maneuvered the Oaks home second in the pennant race in 1946. Among his pitchers that year were Frank (Specs) Shea and Gene Beardon. It turned out that both were property of the Yankees. Shea was shipped to New York in 1947 and helped the Yankees win a pennant for Bucky Harris. The 1946 Oaks got a 15 – 15 performance from Shea and 15 – 4 from Beardon. Between the two, they formed one of the strongest pairs of starting pitchers in the league. Wally Westlake, later an outfielder in the National League, hit .315 as the team posted a 111 – 72 record. Stengel's big hitter was first baseman Les Scarsella, who collected twenty-two homers, drove in ninety-one runs and hit .332. Catcher Bill Raimondi batted an even .300, but did not hit a single homer.

In addition to Shea and Beardon, Stengel pieced together a pitching staff that included Ralph Buxton (10 – 5), Rinaldo Ardizoia (15 – 7), and Floyd Speer (11 – 8). The club finished four games to the rear of champion San Francisco in a red-hot race that set attendance records on both sides of the bay. To Laws' great pleasure, 634,311 fans, an Oakland record, spun through the turnstiles at the tiny Oaks Park. The attendance total was greater than that achieved by some entire Minor Leagues and also exceeded the paid attendance of both Philadelphia and St. Louis in the American League.

There was no question that Stengel had insured himself of a job at Oakland for 1947 and he was inclined to accept. "The first year at Oakland was exciting even for an old man like me, and I was glad to have the opportunity to return to work for Mr. Laws and Mr. Blumenfeld again," the rehired manager said.

However, Stengel's stay in Oakland was to lay the groundwork for his ultimate return to the Major Leagues in what, to many observers, was a most unexpected way and in a most unexpected place.

During the post-war years, construction magnate Del Webb spent a good deal of time in Oakland doing business. Being one of the three new owners of the New York Yankees, Webb naturally went to Oaks Park for many games when the Oakland club was at home. He was favorably impressed with Stengel's juggling of his material. During the course of the 1946 season, Casey used four different men at second base and employed similar strategy at other positions to get as much mileage out of the Oaks' material as possible.

As was his usual form, Stengel was also an energetic promoter of his club and baseball in general. Webb encountered him on more than one occasion in his performances off the field.

"I got to know Casey fairly well," Webb said later. "I was at a party in Oakland one night and Casey was among the guests. He was in rare form. He had us standing around with our mouths open, putting on one of the best shows I've ever seen—telling stories, hopping around the room, mimicking other people. I had an important business appointment early the next morning, so at about 3 A.M., I decided to duck out and catch a couple hours of sleep. When I left, Casey was still holding forth. Well, I got my sleep, not much, but some, and then I staggered out and got a cab to take me to my appointment. We were going past a vacant lot and I looked out and there were a bunch of kids with bats and gloves gathered around an old gaffer who was giving them some instruction. I took another look just to make sure. The old gaffer was my friend Casey. I thought to myself then that if he really cared that much about baseball, he must be a terrific manager."

Having made that kind of an impression on a baseball club owner, particularly one like Del Webb, was not unlikely to produce some positive results. In time, those results were to a shock to many in baseball. Stengel, meanwhile, went into the 1947 season at Oakland with another club that was a mixture of hopefuls and has-beens collected by the skillful Laws. Bearden was among those who returned from the 1946 edition. In 1947, the lefty turned in a 16−7 season and reduced his earned-run average.

In 1946, Bearden worked 167 innings and posted a 3.13 earned-run average. The next season, he pitched 198 innings and his earned-run mark was 2.86. He was clearly ready for a shot at the majors. However, Bearden had struck out only 161 men in those 365 innings, and Stengel felt that he did not possess the fast ball needed to make a consistent winner in the majors. In fact, Stengel had taught Bearden a knuckler to make him more effective for the Oaks. On the strength of Stengel's opinion, the Yankees sold Bearden to Cleveland where he became a twenty-game winner for the champion Indians of 1948. But Stengel's analysis was justified by time, as Bearden never regained that form, and even eventually drifted out of the majors. While Shea was not the overpowering Major League pitcher many thought he might be, either, Stengel was correct when he observed that he was ready for the majors after the 1946 year in which he fanned 124 in 174 innings and posted a 1.66 earned-run average.

Virtually unknown to the press and most baseball men, respect for the Stengel genius was growing behind the scenes at Yankee Stadium. In late 1947, another event that was to influence Stengel's future started in New York when Webb and his partner, Dan Topping, bought out Larry MacPhail and made farm director George Weiss the general manager of the Yankees.

Also of some significance, after the start of the 1947

season, the Oaks picked up a loud-mouth, aggressive twenty-year-old second baseman named Billy Martin. The marriage of Martin and Stengel was to help the Oaks to a 96—90 season and fourth place, with a strong finish. Their collaboration was also to set the table for the 1948 campaign.

The Yankees had won the 1947 pennant for Harris and went on to defeat Brooklyn in the World Series. In 1948, they were not so fortunate. For Stengel, on the other hand, the exact opposite situation occured. After a third-place finish at Oakland in 1947, the Oaks came home first in the Pacific Coast League race in 1948. With Martin playing a key role, the Oaks rolled up a 114—74 record and captured the post-season playoffs to give them a clean sweep of regular-season and playoff honors.

Stengel was the toast of Oakland and the Oaks' owners, Laws and Blumenfeld, gave him a "Casey Stengel Night" at Oaks Park. He was presented with among other things, a new Cadillac.

Contrary to some of the commentary that had accompanied his departure from Boston, Stengel was hailed universally in Oakland by the press and the players, as well as the fans and the Oaks' owners. He had learned many a lesson from his years of experience. He was to employ many of those lessons in his term at Oakland, and they were to help make him successful in many ways. Though still the clown, many of the rough edges had been smoothed by time. As Stengel himself later commented, "I did plenty of things, as a youngster, which I shouldn't have in the majors. If any player ever did those things on my team, I'd have fined his ears off."

Instead of fining the Oakland club, he fed them into the pennant.

His 1948 club was a collection of individualists, as one writer put it. But he forged them into a winning team in every sense of the phrase. Later, one of the veterans on the club disclosed one of Casey's secrets. "If we won a doubleheader, Casey would come in the clubhouse and say, 'You fellas did pretty well today and it's up to me to buy you a three-dollar dinner. The next day, he'd come in with a pocketful of bills and give each of us three bucks. In a playoff game that year we were getting beat, 9−2, and came back and won it, 23−15. It was the darnedest game you ever saw. Afterward Casey said, 'Every man here rates a ten-dollar dinner from the old man.' The next day, he passed out ten bucks apiece to twenty-seven men from his own pocket. No wonder we played our heads off for him.''

By now Stengel was independently wealthy and, in addition, was close to a magnificent baseball triumph at Oakland, and he knew it. He was also not about to permit anything to escape his grasp if he could do anything about it. Stengel may well have given away his entire Oakland salary to the players before that season ended, particularly in view of the fact that the Pacific Coast League in those days played a 190-game schedule. But the money was of little consequence to Casey. He wanted the satisfaction of winning again. He got it, and Oakland had its first pennant since 1927 which, ironically, was also the year Stengel managed his first pennant-winning club, Toledo of the American Association.

On Sunday, October 10, Stengel got a call from George Weiss, who was then in Cleveland attending the World Series between the Indians and the Boston Braves.

"Casey," Weiss said, "we want you to fly to New York and meet us there tomorrow night. If you'd like to manage the Yankees, the job's yours.''

Stengel and Brick Laws took off for New York the next morning and after getting settled in the Waldorf-Astoria, they met with Topping and Weiss. Stengel singed a two-year contract that called for $35,000 per year and he became the fifteenth manager in the history of the New York Yankees.

Once the word leaked out, the voice of Dave Egan was heard in the pages of the Boston *Daily Record*: "Well, sirs and ladies," he wrote. "The Yankees have now been mathematically eliminated from the 1949 pennant race. They eliminated themselves when they engaged Perfesser Casey Stengel to mismanage them for the next two years, and you may be sure that the perfesser will oblige to the best of his unique ability.''

Egan was overreacting, to be sure, but the New York press was hardly overwhelming in its reception of the new

Yankee manager. The general suspicion was that the Yanks had hired Stengel to do his entertaining vaudeville act, to cover up for what was the expected decline in the fortunes of the aging Yankee team and gloss over the firing of the generally popular, though colorless Harris.

As a result, what should have been a joyous occasion for Stengel at the posh 21 Club on October 12, 1948, when the announcement press conference was held, was something of a subdued affair conducted under not one, but several, clouds. The one item of some extreme pleasure to Stengel was that it happened to be an anniversary.

The date of his introduction to the press and public as the new Yankee field boss came twenty-five years to the day after he had beaten the Bombers in a Series game at Yankee Stadium and had thumbed his nose at the infuriated Yanks as he toured the bases. In such things, Stengel often found glee. His life often seemed filled with such odd twists of fate.

CHAPTER 6

Brilliant Buffoon

The rather somber mood of the press conference that announced Stengel's move to the Yankees was followed by perhaps the most serious winter of study in the Ol' Perfessor's life. He realized that the Yankees appointment carried with it several unstated obligations and opportunities.

After a decade as a second-division manager in the National League, he was now thrust into a situation in which his team, built around the brilliant Joe DiMaggio, was capable of winning a pennant. This was a goal Stengel desperately wanted to achieve. Tabbed as a journeyman outfielder with some humorous proclivities by most baseball observers, Casey was anxious to prove, that given some talent, he could manage a winning team without resorting to the comedy antics that had marked his other Major League managerial roles. He also was keenly aware, however, that failure to perform would reflect badly upon his old friend, Yankee general manager George M. Weiss, who had gone somewhat out on a limb in his selection of Stengel to manage the Yankees. He also labored under the handicap of being almost totally unfamiliar with the American League. His term on the Pacific Coast had given him the chance he had hoped and prayed for—one more shot as a big league pilot. He knew it was probably his last.

With all of this weighing on his mind, Stengel prepared himself for the Yankee spring training camp at St. Petersburg, Florida; in every way he was able. Even before the camp opened, the New York press was heavily speculating on how this kooky clown from the National League would fit into with the Yankees and their tradition of stern organization and exceptional achievement.

They were to learn shortly that the Stengel they remembered from Brooklyn and the Boston Braves was mostly a memory. The Yankee spring training of 1949 was a sharp contrast to that of previous seasons which were marked by the almost lackadaisical approach of Bucky

Harris. Stengel and his staff of coaches organized the camp with military precision, a style most often expected of Branch Rickey and other serious students of the game's fine points.

Stengel took the Yankees, with the exception of a few stars, through daily two-a-day workouts that included heavy emphasis on many of the game's subtleties—cutoff plays, pickoffs, fielding bunts, hit-and-runs, squeeze plays. Given the high level of Yankee talent, these drills produced a highly-efficient performance that paid big dividends as the season wore on. The press was somewhat taken aback by what was transpiring. Most were unable to perceive that Stengel would have dearly loved to employ these basic principals with the clubs he had previously managed, had there been any hope of sufficient talent to benefit from them. He had, in fact, used them with more than average impact on his better Minor League clubs.

Despite his valiant efforts, however, the Yankees continued to produce inconsistent performances during the Grapefruit League season. Chilled New Yorkers who waded through the morning cold for their newspaper each day were greeted by box scores that disclosed the uneven nature of the Yankee performance. Some days the team would perform with uncanny excellence. The following day, routine mistakes would bring on a defeat at the hands of an unlikely victor, including an embarrassing defeat by a Minor League club.

One of Stengel's major problems, of course, was the ailing DiMaggio. The off-season operation designed to correct his heel spurs was less than a success. DiMaggio struggled valiantly with the stabbing pain in his feet in the early days of spring training. However, he was quickly dispatched to the sidelines for rest. After days of physical and mental agony, he was pursuaded to return to Johns Hopkins in Baltimore for another operation with the assurance that it would bring an end to the problem. DiMaggio, of course, was haunted by the thought that his career might be coming to a premature close.

Stung a heavy blow by the loss of DiMaggio for an unforeseen period, Stengel began revising his lineups in an effort to find a winning combination without Joltin' Joe. One

CASEY LOOKS INTO THE FUTURE DURING 1949 SEASON.

of his big problems was catching; Larry Berra was clearly a potentially great hitter but a less-than-stellar receiver. He had been sparsely used by Harris because of his defensive deficiencies. Stengel assigned coach Bill Dickey, a Yankee great behind the plate during his career, to develop Berra into a professional Major League catcher.

The infield was another problem. Phil Rizzuto was secure at shortstop, but from there it was anybody's guess what the Yankees would put at the other three positions. Third had been largely the province of Billy Johnson during the Harris years. But Stengel felt that Johnson's lack of speed was a detriment to the Yank attack. His only realistic replacement was the left-swinging Bobby Brown, a super hitter, but an erratic fielder. Second was held down by George (Snuffy) Stirnweiss, an aging veteran, whose best days were clearly behind him. First was a wide open affair with rookie Jack Phillips the early favorite.

Stengel, however, had more than adequate depth in the outfield even given the absence of DiMaggio. Two-thirds of the great outfield of Henrich, DiMaggio, and Keller remained. In Tommy Henrich and Charlie Keller, Stengel had two of baseball's outstanding fielders and clutch hitters at his disposal. He also had young Hank Bauer and Gene Woodling, along with the experienced Johnny Lindell.

Resigned to the absence of DiMaggio, Stengel began attacking his myriad problems with typical organization. He determined to platoon the right-hand hitting Johnson at third with Brown, inserted rookie Jerry Coleman at second, and shifted Henrich from right to first base. The latter move allowed him to employ his additional outfield depth where he could use the talents of Bauer and Lindell against left-hand pitching and Woodling and Keller against righties.

The Yankees shot out of the starting gate after their unimpressive spring training and were in the thick of the fight for first place well into mid-season. But it shortly became apparent that DiMaggio was going to be missed and the Bombers' hopes for a pennant depended in great measure upon the possible return of their superstar.

Meanwhile, DiMaggio remained in a silent turmoil in his New York hotel room, often watching the Yankee games on television. Each morning he gently lifted his legs

WORLD SERIES CHAMPIONS, 1949 NEW YORK YANKEES.

BILL DICKEY, A YANKEE COACH IN 1949 GIVES SOME POINTERS TO YOGI IN SPRING TRAINING.

out of bed and placed them on the floor in the hopes that
the doctors' promise that the pain would disappear had
been fulfilled. Each morning for months, he was disappointed. Then, suddenly, on a bright June morning, it happened. Almost in disbelief, DiMaggio repeated the move-
ments. Then he felt the heel. The pain, as the doctors' had
forecast, was gone.

Almost miraculously, Stengel had one of the great
stars in baseball at his command. The DiMaggio of
mid-1949 would certainly not be the DiMaggio of a decade
earlier, who had terrorized American League pitchers with
his bat and base-runners with his arm, or who had thrilled
Yankee fans with his defensive performances. But his in-
spirational presence would be massive. He could certainly
pinch-hit in clutch situations. Such were Stengel's thoughts
upon learning the news that DiMaggio was returning.

These thoughts were, however, not shared by DiMaggio. After less than a week of workouts, he played in a
Mayor's Trophy game against the Giants. The next day, it
was off to Fenway Park for a crucial series against the Red
Sox, the other leading contender for the flag. DiMaggio
asked Stengel to start the first game of the series on June
28, and the startled Stengel agreed. What transpired
thereafter is one of baseball's great legends. In the three
games, DiMaggio smashed four home runs, drove in nine
runs, and scored five times. The Yankees swept the series
and became a real force in the race.

But injuries continued to dog the Yankees. By
season's end some seventy major mishaps were to strike
the club, sidelining almost every man on the team at some
point. But the Yanks remained in contention or on top all
the way. Henrich was enjoying his greatest season and, in
many ways, had assumed the role of leadership normally
held by the absent DiMaggio. Berra became the catcher
Stengel prayed he would, and the young Coleman was the
sensation of the league, hitting well over .300 and teaming
with Rizzuto to become the league's top double-play com-
bine.

The pitching staff, the heart of Stengel's hopes,
performed the way he needed it to do. Vic Raschi, Allie
Reynolds, and especially bullpen ace Joe Page, delivered

consistently. Despite the adversity of the crippling string of injuries, the Yankees went into the final weekend of the season within a game the first-place Red Sox. The final two-game series would determine the American League club in the World Series. One win in the two games would give the pennant to Boston; a Yankee sweep would put New York in the fall classic. Playing before two overflow crowds in the huge Yankee Stadium, the Bronx Bombers won both games and earned the right to face Brooklyn in the Series.

Like a dream come true, Stengel was managing in the World Series. He made the most of his opportunity, winning the set against his original big league club in five games. Henrich again played a crucial role, as he had throughout the regular season, bashing a home run off Don Newcombe in the ninth inning of the opening game at Yankee Stadium, which gave Vic raschi a 1 − 0 win over Allie Reynolds the next day. But when the Series shifted to Ebbets Field, the Yankees swept three games and closed out the affair. The Bombers built a 10 − 0 lead for Raschi in the fifth game and eased home with a 10 − 6 victory.

The exhausted Yankees were virtually unable to put on the usual victory celebration in the clubhouse after winning the Series. But Stengel was ecstatic. Now his winter was to be much more relaxed, his job secure, Weiss' judgment vindicated. When co-owner Dan Topping succeeded in talking DiMaggio out of retiring, the 1950 campaign looked equally promising.

Having gained the knowledge of the American League he needed, Stengel was much better prepared for the 1950 season. He also had, naturally, an extensive awareness of his own players and their abilities. This led to a continual remodeling of the club as it rolled along to the pennant. In 1949, the Yankees had won ninety-seven games and struggled for the flag. In 1950, the team won ninety-eight games and won with a little more room to spare, again outlasting the Boston club, which was a general pre-season favorite.

Stengel and Weiss began to gradually slough off some of the older Yankees. Keller went to Detroit, Stirnweiss to St. Louis. But one of the important acquisitions was a thirty-seven-year-old former National League home-run

king named Johnny Mize. The huge first baseman was to
play a key role in the Yankee scheme until 1953: he became
the most dangerous pinch-hitter in the American League, a
sometime regular first baseman, an almost-perennial World
Series hero, and a close friend of Stengel. Often he would
sit on the bench during games and give an analysis of the
hitting weaknesses of his teammates. A studious observer
of batting, Mize's thoughts were not always welcome, but
were almost invariably accurate.

But the most important acquisition during 1950 was the
mid-season rookie arrival, left-hand pitcher Eddie Ford.
Ford was 9−1 during the second half of the campaign and
he virtually insured the Yanks of the title with his almost
flawless performance. When the surprising Philadelphia
Phillies won the National League pennant, the Yankees
were up against a team that had not been in the post-season
event since 1915. But the Whiz Kids found the Series
almost anticlimactic after their hysterical victory in the
pennant race against Brooklyn.

The Yanks were confident, cool, and without a doubt
superior to the Phillies. Even the surprise of relief ace Jim
Konstanty on the mound as the starter for the Phils in the
opening game at Shine Park did little to ruffle the demeanor
of the Bombers, who raced through the series in four
straight wins.

Stengel had now won two pennants and two Series in
two years. Weiss and his bosses, Dan Topping and Del
Webb, could now be more than pleased with their selection
of the left-handed former dental student as their field boss.
Yet, for the Yankee owners and the team's fans, the best
was yet to come.

Scout Tom Greenwade had signed a young prodigy
from Oklahoma the same year Stengel inked his first
Yankee contract. In a sense, both Stengel and Mickey Mantle were to become part of the Yankee legend together. It
was under Stengel that Mantle was to mature into his great-
ness, and after his departure, Mantle enjoyed one super
season and then a long steady decline.

The two men first confronted one another at Phoenix,
Arizona, in 1951 when the spring training camp opened.
Mantle had had the misfortune of arriving on the tailwind of

an enormous press buildup. He had been hailed as the replacement for DiMaggio as leader of the Yankees. Unfortunately, DiMaggio had decided to play one final season, and Mantle was a shy backcountry kid. The chemistry could not have been worse. After a pressure-cooker spring training, Mantle came to New York and was overwhelmed by both the city and the press. By midseason, Mantle was farmed out to Kansas City to get himself back together. Late in the season, he returned to the Yankees and Stengel made him a personal project.

In the midst of all of the internal furor, the Yankees merrily rolled along and won their third straight pennant for Stengel. In the Series, DiMaggio and Mantle were once again teamed up in the outfield with DiMaggio in his accustomed place in center and the heir-apparent patrolling right. The opposition, this time, was the surprising New York Giants, who had snatched the pennant from the Dodgers in the hysterical ninth-inning playoff game rally that made Bobby Thomson immortal.

But the Yankees made plenty of news of their own during 1951, before the spotlight shifted to the Dodger – Giant race that closed out the National League season with a rush. Reynolds was one of the big headline makers, pitching two no-hitters. The first was against his first Major League club, Cleveland, and the second clinched the pennant against Boston at Yankee Stadium. The second had a storybook finish when Ted Williams fouled to Berra for the final out in the ninth and Berra dropped the ball. Williams then fouled the next pitch in almost the same spot, and Yogi caught it for the final out.

Stengel's achievement of managing his club to the pennant marked the first time in nearly half a century that a manager had won three titles during his first three years in a league. But Stengel became a record all unto himself when the Yankees disposed of the Giants in six games to win their third straight Series. Mantle's return enabled him to play in the Series, but he stepped on a Yankee Stadium drain cap and wrenched his knee in the second game of the Series. He did not play again until the next year.

The end of the 1951 Series also marked the close of DiMaggio's glorious Yankee career. He retired with a

lifetime. .325 batting average and was subsequently named
the "Greatest Living Player" during baseball's centennial
in 1969.

Stengel's personal involvement with Mickey Mantle
became almost crucial to the Yankees when the 1952 campaign drew near. While Casey was publicly asking the question as to who was going to replace the great DiMaggio in
the role as the Yankee leader, he knew deep inside what the
answer had to be. Yet, in an effort to deflect some of the
pressure from Mantle, Stengel would rattle off a list of
names . . . Berra . . . rookies Bob Cerv and Jackie
Jensen . . . some other fellow . . . in his own inimitable
style.

Mantle did, indeed, become the Yankee leader, but
such was not initially the case, and Stengel did a good deal
of maneuvering in the early part of the season to get the
Yankees going in pursuit of their fourth straight pennant.

Billy Martin emerged as a sparkplug at second base;
young Gil MacDougald returned to third base after having
been shifted to second in place of Coleman (who was back
in the service); Joe Collins became the first-base regular,
and Bauer developed into the regular right-fielder. Berra
was now established as a legitimate star, perhaps the best
clutch hitter in the American League. With Ford also in the
service, Reynolds and Raschi continued to be the
mainstays of the pitching staff, along with junkman Eddie
Lopat. But both were beginning the decline that was to end
their careers.

Mantle hit .311 and slammed tape-measure home runs.
Casey pieced the pitching together, and the Yankees
notched another flag. In the Series, the Yanks faced the
strong challenge of the Dodgers, who had finally shaken off
the string of weird finishes that had cost them pennants on
the final day of play for two successive years.

Perhaps the finest of all the post-war Brooklyn power-
houses, the 1952 Dodgers were a strong challenge to the
Yankees, and the Series turned out to be a hard-fought
seven-game adventure that the Yanks finally won, 4−2, at
Ebbets Field. Billy Martin saved the game with a long dash
to catch a bases-loaded popup by Jackie Robinson that had
been lost in the sun by the rest of the Yankee infield.

THE YANKEE CLIPPER, JOE DIMAGGIO.

Martin had been for a long time a pet of Stengel's for just such reasons. He always made the clutch play. Stengel's many years in baseball had taught him the value of talent on the field, regardless of the personal idiosyncrasies of its possessor. Martin had first joined Stengel in Oakland and played for the Pacific Coast League championship club Casey had managed before signing with the Yankees. It was with some irony, then, that this often controversial man, who was two decades later to become a Yankee manager himself, earned Stengel his fourth straight Series title. The four straight championships matched the record set by another Yankee managerial great, Joe McCarthy, in the 1930s.

The record was destined to be broken by Stengel's club the following year. In 1953 the Yankee machine was beginning to assert what seemed to be an almost total dominance of the American League. Chicago, Cleveland, and Boston had been modest contenders in the late 1940s and early 1950s, but only Cleveland (1948) was to disrupt the Yankee chain from 1947 to 1954 when the Indians did it again. But, in 1953, the Yankees were to retain their dominance.

Mantle's continued emergence as a star was paramount to the Yankee success, but it was by no means the entire story. Stengel's juggling around the drafting of his men for service in the Korean War was of equal import to the success.

By 1953, much of the juggling became unnecessary. For the first time since he became the Yankee manager, Stengel had a full deck. Ford returned from the service to join Lopat, Raschi, and Reynolds. In the infield were Colling, Martin, Rizzuto, and McDougald. Outfielders included Mantle, Bauer, Woodling, and Irv Noren, acquired from Washington. Berra, naturally, was the catcher.

The Yankees won the pennant and the Series, defeating Brooklyn in six games. Stengel thus entered a class all unto himself. No manager in the history of the game had ever won five straight pennants and five straight World Series with a team or in a league.

In 1954, the Yankees won more games (103) than any other Stengel club had done. But they failed to win a pennant. The law of averages, perhaps as much as any other factor, saw the Cleveland Indians win an American League record 111 games. New Yorkers gained some measure of satisfaction when their Giants swept the Indians in four straight in the Series. But Stengel was distraught, and he blamed himself for allowing complacency to overtake the Yankees. He would not make the same mistake again during the ensuing years of his tenure in the Bronx ballyard.

During the course of his first five years at the helm of the Yankees, Stengel was both a participant and a witness to some of the more far-reaching developments in this history of the Yankee club and baseball in general. The club that he had inherited in 1948 was largely the residue of many years of Joe McCarthy's stewardship on the field and Ed Barrow's in the front office. The team was built around the superlative DiMaggio, and the supporting cast had grown accustomed to the ways of McCarthy. Bucky Harris had really done little to alter the previous pattern, preferring to continue the habits of the McCarthy regime.

One of the incidents that came almost at the dawning moment of Stengel's Yankee career was the creation of the $100,000 ballplayer. The man involved was, of course, DiMaggio. In 1947, the Yankees were owned by the triumvirate of Larry MacPhail, Dan Topping, and Del Webb. The trio had just purchased the club the year before from the estate of the late Jacob Ruppert. Ruppert had died in 1939, but the onslaught of World War II precluded any action by the estate before 1946. In the interim, general manager Barrow became the de facto owner and operator of the team. Barrow, with his long business background in baseball, was not exactly notorious for his largess in dealing with the players. As a result, DiMaggio was making only $32,000 in 1947, when Barrow and MacPhail had their first conversation about DiMaggio's future.

Topping and Webb, in the meanwhile, were finding that serving as partners with the dynamic MacPhail was not exactly to their liking, and they determined to end the tripartite arrangement. MacPhail was unable to buy them out, so Topping and Webb acquired all of the Yankee stock and Topping, a former pro football promoter, became the team's president and active owner.

Though DiMaggio had no way of knowing it, Topping

was a big DiMaggio fan. He raised Joltin' Joe to $75,000 for
1948, and when DiMaggio asked for $100,000 for 1949, Top-
ping readily agreed. One of the reasons for his agreement
was the potential publicity value of having baseball's first
$100,000 ballplayer. Topping believed that, in business as
well as in the ballpark, the Yankees should be baseball's
leaders. Some other facts undoubtedly entered into Topping's thinking at the same time. One was that the Yankees
had drawn a staggering 2,373,901 at the gates (a club record
that still stands) in 1948. Another was the anticipated
favorable press which the event might help to obscure the
announcement of the firing of Harris and the subsequent
hiring of Stengel.

The friendship between Topping and DiMaggio grew
and Topping was able to talk his star out of retiring when
Joe seriously considered it after the 1950 season. Stengel's
view of the DiMaggio situation was somewhat different. It
was obvious to all (including DiMaggio) that his best playing days were behind him. His big league career began in
1936 with forecasts that his bad legs would prevent him
from ever becoming a superstar despite his enormous
achievements with the San Francisco Seals of the Pacific
Coast League. It was now fifteen years later, and DiMaggio's record was massive.

Stengel, however, realized that as long as DiMaggio remained with the Yankees, he would serve as the tangible
link with the McCarthy regime, preventing him from mold-
ing the team in his own image and fully enforcing his stamp
upon the Yankees. DiMaggio, for instance, was among the
select few players permitted to travel by train when the
Yanks flew from city to city. The so-called "Cinder Set"
moving independently of the main body of the team was an
annoyance to Stengel.

It indicated to the writers making the trips that Stengel
did not have DiMaggio under his complete direction. The
others in the same category were also immune from
Stengel's hand as long as they were able to travel under the
cloak of DiMaggio's protection. The same problem confronted Weiss for much the same reasons. But the close-
ness of Topping and DiMaggio also precluded any action on

SHORTSTOP PHIL RIZZUTO.

THE BIG CAT, JOHNNY MIZE.

his part, as the general manager explained to Stengel, anytime the subject came up.

This and other minor problems were bothersome to the manager who could do little but endure them as long as the Yankee Clipper was the team leader. Since DiMaggio's effectiveness as a player was diminished, Stengel had hoped Topping would be unable to talk him out of retiring. This was particularly true since Stengel secretly believed that Mantle would be the next superstar who could enable the Bronx Bombers to continue their domination of the American League.

Shortstop Phil Rizzuto, and others from the earlier eras of McCarthy and Harris, were also prone to be distrusted by Stengel, and he sought to reduce their ranks through trades and to steadily increase the number of men on the team whose total exposure to the Yankees was under him.

When DiMaggio retired after the 1951 season, Stengel publicly joined in the gracious and adultating praise of him. But inwardly he was pleased that the problem had finally resolved itself, and he could now get full and total control of the club and its on-field destinies. By 1952, the Yankees had begun to become what Stengel had prayed for: his team, with him as the acknowledged boss and Mantle as the emerging leader.

Mantle was indeed the fulfillment of Stengel's dream and his huge talent, despite his constant battle with injuries, was the fuel that powered the Yanks. The fact that DiMaggio played the 1951 season put two of the greatest outfielders in baseball on the field at the same time. Mantle, largely, played right field that season, with DiMaggio retaining his position of honor in center. The one-season overlap also maintained the unique string that extended from 1920 to 1968 in which the Yankees continuously had one (or more) giant superstars on their team. Babe Ruth joined the Bombers in 1920, Lou Gehrig in 1925, DiMaggio in 1936, and Mantle in 1951. Gehrig played on several teams with Ruth, DiMaggio on several with Gehrig, Mantle on one with DiMaggio. Mantle's retirement in 1968 brought a final conclusion to the streak that was probably unequalled anywhere in pro sports' history.

The continuous string of Yankee superstars, plus their more-than-competent supporting casts, enabled the club to cast a giant shadow over the American League. When Stengel first came to the Yanks, the principal contenders for the top spot were the Indians and Red Sox, who had tied for the pennant the year before (1948) with Cleveland winning the one-game playoff at Fenway Park. The Yankees' dramatic 1949 pennant victory started a five-year string during which time the Boston and Cleveland clubs declined somewhat, and the Red Sox declined more dramatically. Cleveland remained strong largely because of its deep pitching staff which during the period included such names as Bob Feller, Bob Lemon, Early Wynn, and Mike Garcia. The Red Sox were centered around perhaps the greatest pure hitter of the era, Ted Williams.

Williams was supported by a cast of aging veterans including second baseman Bobby Doerr, third baseman Vern Stephens, and DiMaggio's brother, Dominic, the center fielder. However, neither Boston nor Cleveland was able to match the continuing flow of young talent that Yankee scouts steadily poured into the farm system. When men of the caliber of Doerr, Stephens, and DiMaggio retired, the Red Sox were unable to replace them. When DiMaggio left the Yankees, Mantle stepped into his place and joined a club that already included such outstanding players as Whitey Ford (then in military service), Hank Bauer, Gene Woodling, Vic Raschi, Yogi Berra, and Allie Reynolds.

A new force was developing in Chicago where the long-moribund White Sox had put together a new management team consisting of Frank Lane and Paul Richards. Lane, who quickly earned the nickname "Trader," swapped off almost every warm body on the Sox roster for new (and younger) faces like Jim Rivera, Minnie Minoso, Nelson Fox, Chico Carresquel, and a few established stars like George Kell and Eddie Robinson. Richards rebuilt the pitching staff and turned the team into a collection of running jackrabbits. Dubbed the "Go-Go Sox" by their fans, the White Sox suddenly became a pennant contender in 1951 and gave the Yanks a brief run for their money. But throughout the early 1950s, Chicago was able to do little more than make fragile bids for the flag. Lane and Richards had neither the depth nor the farm system to seriously compete with the Yankees.

Lane inveigled Detroit into selling him left-hander Billy Pierce, who became the spine of the Chicago pitching staff. Stengel generally made a practice of pitching Ford against Pierce. These encounters seemed invariably to produce 1−0 wins for Ford. But one of the more bizarre defeats the Yankees hung on Pierce came on July 28, 1954, at Chicago's Comiskey Park. The White Sox jumped out to a big early lead, 6−0, before the Yankees got perking. Weather also became a factor, as did Stengel. With Chicago leading, 6−1, a drenching rain started. The field was covered, the game delayed, the field uncovered, and the game resumed. The Yankees then scored three runs in the eighth inning before another rain interruption. Into the ninth, it was once more raining and the umpires called a halt to the proceedings. Hank Bauer had opened the inning with a single through the middle and Irv Noren singled to right. Jim Rivers charged through the water in right and rifled a throw to third, where Bauer was called safe in a close play. During the argument over the call, the rain caused still another delay.

The umpires seriously considered ending the game, even with the tying runs aboard, when Stengel began a raucous protest that led them to agree to permit the game to continue. Mantle was the next hitter due for the Yankees and after the Chicago pitcher had completed his warmup pitches, Richards slowly made his way to the mound and called for a relieve pitcher, obviously hoping the stall would bring on more rain and end the debacle with Chicago in front, 6−4. Slowly, the new Sox pitcher ambled in from the bullpen in deep center. When he removed his jacket, it was none other than Billy Pierce. After he, in turn, warmed up, Mantle stepped into the box and slammed the first pitch into the lower deck of the left-field. The Yankees then swung at pitches they could not hit with a broom and raced onto the field.

Stengel brought in one of his insurance policies, so thoughtfully provided by George Weiss, to pitch in the ninth inning. Johnny Sain, once one of the two aces of the 1948 pennant-winning Boston Braves, worked quickly

THE FIRST YANKEE CATCHER THAT WORE
NUMBER EIGHT, BILL DICKEY.

against the threatening weather and the White Sox. Sain retired the first two men before Fox dropped a wind-blown
double into the mud between Noren and Mantle. Then he
disposed of Minoso to end the game.

The Yankees did not win the pennant in 1954, but
games of that type left a lasting impression on opposing
teams and their fans. The Yankees had become the leading
drawing card in baseball when Ruth joined the team in 1920.
They remained so throughout their entire era of dominance.
The fact that the Yankees represented the nation's largest
city, and they always carried both the winning tradition and
the top stars, provided them with an almost unbeatable gate
appeal.

While the stars sold the tickets, both at home and on
the road, it was the balance of the squad that, as often as
not, played crucial roles in key games. Stengel was a master
at maneuvering his bench strength, and Weiss always saw
to it that he had a bench to work with. When he became the
field manager of the original Mets in 1962, Stengel made a
regular out of forty-year-old Gene Woodling. This was really nothing more than a throwback to his use of John Mize as
a part-time and pinch-hitter par excellence with the
Yankees of the early 1950s. While he was with the
Yankees, Woodling was almost entirely a platoon man. So
was Hank Bauer, though, for exactly the opposite reason;
Bauer was a righty hitter.

But Stengel's real mastery was his psychology with the
boys who were not playing. Certain players need constant
needling and must be driven by a steady whip of criticism.
Others must be complimented and have their hands held.
Stengel knew what each man needed and also how to best
achieve his desired results. When a platoon ballplayer got
into a game for Stengel, he always gave his best (and then
some) since he hoped to at least retain what status he
already had if not improve some and get more playing time.

Stengel's psychology evidenced itself in other ways,
too. When the Yankees fell into one of their occasional losing streaks, he would rarely call a clubhouse meeting. The
high level of performance expected of the players weighed
heavily in those days; they were well aware of their abilities
and the need to halt the habits that may have brought on the

**BILLY MARTIN ACCEPTS MANAGER'S HUG IN DRESSING ROOM
AFTER 1952 YANKEES CLINCHED PENNANT.**

streak. But once the club won a game, Stengel was likely to call a meeting in which he would review the entire situation in very earthy, Anglo-Saxon terms. During a winning streak, on the other hand, the manager was often almost impossible to communicate with in any way. He would become enraged at the smallest mistakes and castigate players for any malfeasance, knowing that while a team is winning, it can easily slough off criticism. This trait reached its apex during the 1953 season when the Bombers virtually wrecked the American League with an eighteen-game winning streak that began in late May. As the streak reached epic proportions, Stengel became a total tyrant, roaring and ranting before, during, and after every game. He felt that teams could learn much more in victory than in defeat.

The eighteen-game streak was the longest during the Stengel regime at Yankee Stadium. It should have insured the Yankees the 1953 pennant by the end of June. But the long schedule of baseball is ultimately its own compensating balance. The .450 hitter in May will almost invariably wind up close to his lifetime average, even if that is .220. The Yankees ran into a nine-game losing stretch before the end of June and, suddenly, there was a pennant race again. Their lead cut to five games, the Yankees broke the losing streak and turned it around, ultimately winning the flag by a margin of eight and a half games over Cleveland. It was the largest margin by which the Yankees won any of their first five pennants under Stengel. The margins during the preceding four victorious campaigns had been by one, three, five, and two games.

Perhaps it was the eighteen-game winning streak that turned off the fans, or the comfortable margin the Yankees maintained during the season, or the absence of DiMaggio before the complete development of Mantle as the superstar he was to become. But for whatever reasons, the steadily-declining attendance at Yankee Stadium hit 1,537,811. During the next seven years of the Stengel rule, attendance was to run at the 1,500,000 level, except for 1960, when it climbed back up to 1,627,349.

From the time Stengel came to the majors in 1912 until his retirement after fifty-four seasons in 1965, no big league club he was associated with was able to win 103 games in a season. The 1954 Yankees had achieved that figure, but they still failed to win the pennant race. Alphonso Lopez, who was to be Stengel's only nemesis, piloted the Indians to the pennant.

Lopez turned the trick of beating a Stengel-managed Yankee team by setting an American League record for victories with 111. Lopez was to earn another pennant in 1959 with the Chicago White Sox, with but ninety-four wins. But Stengel captured all other pennants from 1949 to 1960.

Lopez was a master strategist who lacked the personnel of Stengel's arsenal at New York. But he was an outstanding coach of pitchers and the Indians won primarily on the strength of their pitching. The same was true of the White Sox of 1959. All Lopez needed besides pitching was enough power to score a few runs. Given a small margin, Lopez and his hurlers would do the rest. He developed a bullpen tandem of Ray Narleski and Don Mossi as a lefty-righty combination that proved more than effective on most occasions. The Indian power came from Larry Doby and Al Rosen for the most part. Second baseman Bobby Avila was to win the Most Valuable Player in 1954 for his timely hitting and the league batting title. But defense was hardly the long suit at Municipal Stadium. The infield of the Indians was caustically dubbed the "leaky roof" by local sportswriters.

Once the pitching broke down, the Indians were in trouble. That was what caused their startling downfall at the hands of the New York Giants in the 1954 World Series. The Tribe hurlers were unable to consistently extinguish the Giants bats, particularly that of pinch-hitter Dusty Rhodes.

Thus, the first era of Stengel's years with the Yankees drew to a close on what was, for him, a particularly unhappy note. He got involved in a two-team race for the pennant as the Indians and Yankees literally ran away from the field in the American League, but he finished second in that two-team affair. The fate of the Yankees was sealed on Sunday, September 12, when they dropped both ends of a crucial doubleheader to the Indians before the largest crowd in baseball history (84,587) at Municipal Stadium. During the

second game (which the Yanks lost, 3—2) the crowd
gleefully roared "choke up, choke up" as Cleveland pulled
eight and a half games in front of New York.

The Indians finally won the flag by eight games.

There were several factors that contributed to the
Yankees' failure to win their sixth straight pennant for
Stengel in 1954. One of them was the retirement of the
hard-hitting Bobby Brown in mid-season when he began
the medical internship that ultimately led to his career as
one of the country's finest heart specialists. Another was
the advancing age of several key men on the club, including
shortstop Rizzuto and pitchers Raschi and Reynolds. At
the close of the 1954 season, Stengel was sixty-five years
old. He was uncertain, despite his amazing managing record for the Yankees, that he was even going to be retained
by Weiss.

But once he learned that he was, indeed, going to be
the pilot of the Bombers in 1955, Stengel conferred with
Weiss on ways of solving their problems. A major rebuilding was to take place and many old faces would be either
gone, or on their way out by 1955. Stengel was also banking
on Mantle. "That fella is going to be even greater than now,
and he can make everybody forget about everybody." He
was almost right, close enough to win five pennants in the
next six seasons.

CHAPTER 7

Farewell to Dynasty

As disappointed as Stengel was by the Yankees' failure to sustain their streak of championship seasons in 1954, he was elated by the news that he was to be retained as field manager.

In spite of his age, Stengel felt that he still had a long and fruitful career in baseball ahead of him. Events were to prove him completely correct.

"I never felt old at sixty-five," he once told an interviewer. "In fact, I haven't really ever felt what you could ordinarily call old." At the time he made those remarks, Casey Stengel was eighty-three, and he was on hand to play an active part in Old Timers' Day ceremonies for the Mets at Shea Stadium.

When the 1955 season drew near, there was considerable speculation on whether Yankee dominance in the majors was at an end. After five successive pennants and accompanying World Series victories, the Yanks had been dethroned by a Cleveland club that virtually had its entire lineup returning. The team was highly rated despite its almost unbelievable defeat by the New York Giants in the 1954 Series.

Preseason forecasts rated other clubs in the American League somewhat stronger than they actually proved to be. Many newspapermen felt that 1955 was to be the year for the Chicago White Sox. However, the Yankees won the pennant, finishing three games ahead of the Indians. The White Sox were third.

What was to develop with the Yankee club was actually somewhat more remarkable than their final standings in the American League which, after all, was not so unusual. Feeling that Stengel was correct in his concern about the age of the club members, Weiss set out to do something about it.

Paul Richards, formerly the field boss in Chicago, had been replaced by Marty Marion in mid-1954. Richards subsequently moved to Baltimore to control of the baseball operation there as field manager and de facto general manager. Weiss had an eye on two young Oriole pitchers and Richards wanted to make a big splash in his new position. The situation was ripe for Weiss. He began working with Richards in an effort to pry from Baltimore Bob Turley, a strong-armed right-hander.

The two negotiated until finally, they had constructed the largest package in baseball history—a seventeen-man deal in which nine Yankees and New York farmhands went to Baltimore in exchange for eight Orioles of varying degrees of competence. In many ways, the massive trade was beneficial to both sides. Richards was able to achieve his objective of cleaning house in Baltimore, while Weiss picked up not only one young pitcher (Turley) but a second (Don Larsen) as a bonus. Larsen proved to be a bonus that was to pay one massive dividend. The first portions of the swap were announced on November 18, 1954, although the deal was not formally completed until December 3.

Although vital, Turley and Larsen were just the start. Weiss sent outfielder Gene Woodling to Baltimore; pitchers Harry Byrd, Bill Miller, and Jim McDonald; catchers Hal Smith and Gus Triandos; and infielders Kal Segrist, Don Leppert, and Willie Miranda. Richards gave New York, in addition to Turley and Larsen, pitcher Mike Blyzka, outfielders Jim Fridley and Ted del Guerico, catcher Darrell Johnson, and infielders Dick Kryhoski and Billy Hunter. Hunter was a utilityman for Stengel and, by virtue of living in the same northern New Jersey area, Johnson became Mickey mantle's chauffeur. But it was Turley and Larsen that Weiss was after; it was they who were to be the main benefits of the deal.

Another significant change, this perhaps of longer-lasting consequence, occurred in spring training. Elston Howard, converted from the outfield to catching, was voted the 1954 Most Valuable Player in the International League on the strength of his .330 batting average and 109 runs-batted in total at Toronto. Under normal circumstances, Howard would have been considered a shoo-in to make the varsity in 1955. However, Howard was black and no black had ever played for the Yankees. Elston Howard was to be the first.

AUTHOR OF THE WORLD SERIES PERFECT GAME, DON LARSEN.

Stengel's enthusiasm for black players was, to be charitable, limited. Having been associated with Major League baseball since 1912, this was probably understandable. But Stengel was also a shrewd baseball man with a sharp eye for talent. A man could have three eyes and one hand and could play for Casey Stengel if he was good enough. Howard was more than good enough. It is likely that Weiss and Stengel would have resisted, or at least ignored, the outcry in the press over the absence of blacks on the Yankees team if they did not feel Howard could cut the mustard. But his ability made keeping him easy.

The 1955 pennant race turned out just about the way it was supposed to. It was, for a large part of the campaign, a four-way race involving half of the circuit. Boston, Chicago, Cleveland, and the Yankees all had legitimate shots at the flag at some point along the way. Boston was the least serious contender of the three, with Cleveland and Chicago each spending a good deal of time in first place during August and September before the Yankees finally took command with a last-second rescue from Billy Martin.

Although unable to play after September 16 because of a torn leg muscle, Mantle drove in ninety-nine runs and led the American League in homers for the first of four times with thirty-seven. Berra proved to be a most effective back-up hitter behind Mantle, forcing opposing pitchers to work to the dynamite switch-hitter more often than they would have liked.

But Mantle's injury was not the only one suffered by a key man in the Yankee club before the season ended. It was, in fact, injuries that made the Yankees vulnerable and gave the opposing clubs a realistic shot at the flag. When the season opened, Stengel had Bill Skowron and Joe Collins alternating at first base, Gerry Coleman at second, Rizzuto at short, and Andy Carey at third. Mantle's outfield mates included Bauer, Woodling, Slaughter, and Irv Noren. Berra, supported by the rookie Howard, was the catcher. The pitching staff included Ford, Tommy Byrne, Turley, Larsen, Bob Grim, Lopat, and rookie Johnny Kucks as starters with Tom Morgan and former Phillie star Jim Konstanty in the bullpen.

At one point early in the campaign, both Skowron and

Collins were in the hospital at the same time. The Yankee bench then produced veteran Eddie Robinson.

Robinson, a journeyman with some power, suddenly became one of the hottest bats in the American League, smashing fifteen homers before July 1. In fact, Robinson was so hot that when Collins was released from the hospital, Stengel inserted him into the outfield.

Injuries dogged the Yanks all season long, but their reserve strength was generally sufficient to keep the Yankees in or near first place until September 1 when Chicago briefly took the lead before beginning their annual swan dive. Cleveland then moved into the top spot until the Yankees were augmented by the addition of Martin, who joined the club almost immediately upon his release from military service.

The pitching staff started exceptionally, with the performance of Larsen being the only major disappointment. He was finally shipped out to Denver. Turley slumped badly after his magnificent start, and it was left up to a pair of left-handers, Ford and Byrne, to carry the load. Byrne was the exact opposite of the poised and workmanlike Ford. He was prone to nonstop conversation on and off the mound. He was also a super lefty hitter who on occasion was used as a pinchhitter by Stengel.

But the Yankees really jelled after Martin's return. Coleman had been replaced at second by Gil MacDougald. When Martin rejoined the team, MacDougald was shifted to third, and the slumping Carey was benched. With but ten games remaining in the season, the Yankees recaptured first place during a series with the Red Sox in New York. They never lost it. Their triumph matched them in the Series with the Brooklyn Dodgers, a team they had met and beaten four times since 1947.

Much to Sengel's disappointment, the 1955 Series didn't produce the expected result of a Yankee-Brooklyn encounter. The Dodgers won. But the way the Series started, such a result was hardly to be anticipated. The Yankees won the opening game on September 28 at Yankee Stadium, 6−5, and duplicated their win with another the next day, 4−2, before the scene shifted to Brooklyn's Ebbets Field.

Once back in the friendly confines of their own ballyard, the Dodgers came to life, sweeping three games by
scores of $8-3$, $8-5$, and $5-3$. When the two teams came
back to the Stadium, the Yankees needed to win both of the
two remaining games to take the Series. They got the first
one on October 3, $5-1$. The seventh and decisive game was
a tough, tense defensive struggle that matched young
southpaw Johnny Podres of Brooklyn against the Yanks'
Turley. Turley only allowed five hits, but Gil Hodges
reached him for two runs batted in, one off a sacrifice fly.
Podres scattered eight hits and was salvaged by a remarkable catch in the leftfield corner by Sandy Amoros when
Yogi Berra's drive looked like extra bases. Worse for
Stengel and the Yankees, the lefty-fielding Amoros was
able to get the ball back into the infield fast enough to turn
his circus catch into a double play that broke the back of a
Yankee potential rally. Podres held on from there to win,
$2-0$, giving the Dodgers their first Series after seven un-
successful tries beginning in 1916.

The Yankees' reasonably comfortable win in 1955 left
Stengel and Weiss with little preparatory work, other than
the usual minor adjustments. They had confidence in Ford,
who had tied for the American League lead in victories during his $18-7$ season in 1955, and most of their other
pitching.

Following their Series defeat, the Yankees had a trip
which most of the players did not want to make. They went
to Japan. But, for Stengel, the twenty-four-game exercise
was a unique opportunity to assess his troops. His competitive instincts brought him to lecture the club about the
trip before it began. He told his men, "I expect 100 percent
from every man in every game on this here trip, and remember I will be watching." The message was clear: Your
job in 1956 in New York might well depend on your performance in 1955 in Japan.

With his inspiring admonition ringing in their years, the
Yanks went out sailing in every game. They won twenty-
three times; the other game was a tie.

Several of the players materially benefited from the
playing time they received during the trip. The only regular
who didn't go was Phil Rizzuto, left behind because his

YANKEE LEFTHANDER WHITEY FORD.

**GREATEST SWITCH HITTER
OF ALL TIME, MICKEY MANTLE.**

wife, Cora, was pregnant. Stengel used a MacDougald at short during much of the trip and his play was so good that the aging Rizzuto became expendable. He was released during the 1956 season. Pitcher Johnny Kucks learned how to throw a slider from pitching coach Jim Turner. Andy Carey smacked thirteen homers in the twenty-four games and was determined to become a power hitter. This judgment was never shared by Stengel and contributed to Carey's demise as a hitter and the ultimate shortening of his career.

The 1956 spring training was not remarkable, but when the season opened on April 17 at Washington's Griffith Stadium, the Yankees gave the American League a preview of what it was in for during the season. Mantle smashed two gigantic homers over the center-field wall in the spacious old Washington park, driving in four runs. Berra was four-for-four with a homer and five runs batted in.

Stengel's crew charged out of the starting gate with seven wins in the first eight games and moved into first place on May 3, where they were to remain for all but two days during the entire balance of the schedule. Cleveland held the lead for two days following a 3−2 win by Bob Lemon and a rainout. But on May 16, the Yankees won the finale of the Indian series to regain the first-place position that they never relinquished again. By June 1, they had stretched their margin out to-six-and-a-half games over Chicago, which by now had taken over second place from Cleveland.

On June 15, they started a seven-game winning streak. Mantle was continuing his incredible hitting with Berra, MacDougald, and Showron not far off his pace. Ford was humming along beyond Stengel's expectations. Some of the older pitchers, notable Tommy Byrne, and Mickey McDermott, an off-season acquisition from the Senators, were substantial disappointments. Bob Grim developed a bad arm. But Kucks, armed with his new slider, became the second starter behind Ford. Meanwhile, Detroit unwittingly did the Yankees a favor. Stengel asked Weiss to send young Tom Sturdivant out to Denver for additional Minor League work. But the Tigers refused waivers on Sturdivant, forcing the Yanks to keep him. With Byrne,

McDermott, and Grim having unproductive years, Sturdivant became a starting regular.

Stengel received something of a jolt in late June. The
Yankees went roaring into Chicago only to be swept in a
four-game series by the White Sox. The four wins enabled
the Sox to cut the Yankee lead to but one game and allowed
third-place Cleveland to crawl within four and a half games.
But the Yankees then won eighteen of their next twenty
games to pull away from the pack again, with Mantle hitting
another hot streak.

Mantle was the talk of baseball and was developing a
legitimate threat to Babe Ruth's record of sixty homers in a
season. He was also accomplishing unusual feats. On July
1, during a doubleheader sweep of the Senators, he switch-
hit homers in the second game. It was the second time that
season he had accomplished this unique achievement and
the fourth time in his career. The homers, as Mantle's so
often were, also were significant in enabling the Yankees to
win. With the Bombers trailing, 6−5, in the seventh, the
switcher unloaded a tremendous shot off Dean Stone batting right-handed, which tied the score. On his next trip to
the place in the ninth, Mantle batted lefty against Bud
Byerly and socked the ball into the Yankee bullpen in right-
center with a man on for an 8−6 victory.

Shortly after this demonstration by Mantle, the
Yankees started still another winning skein, this to reach
eleven games, their longest such run of the season. One of
the key points in the streak came on July 15 when the
Yanks beat Chicago both ends of a doubleheader. Ford
won the first game, 2−1, over Billy Pierce. Kucks won the
second game in relief, 6−5, in ten innings. Kucks started
and won a shutout on July 17, 4−0 over Detroit. The
Tigers' Paul Foytack snapped the string, 8−4, the next
day.

The winning streak ballooned the Yank first-place
margin back into double figures. But it was cut sharply
again when a losing streak started on July 31, with three defeats in a row being administered by both Cleveland and
Detroit. Stengel then reached into the Yankee farm system
for some pitching help. He asked Weiss to give him young
right-hander Ralph Terry from Denver. In his Major

League debut on August 6, Terry beat Boston, 4—3, to snap the skid.

Ironically, Terry lost his next two starts and was sent back to Denver.

The pennant-clinching came on September 18 in an almost storybook circumstance. The event took place at Comiskey Park with Ford downing Pierce, 3—2, in an eleven-inning thriller. Mantle supplied the winning run with his fiftieth homer of the season. The win was Ford's nineteenth. He lost his bid for his first twentieth-win season when he dropped a heartbreaking 1—0 decision to rookie Charlie Beamon on September 26 at Baltimore in his only start after the pennant-clinching victory. In the pitching, one of the more remarkable events in the closing weeks of the season was the turnaround of Don Larsen. The flaky right-hander, who had once been sent back to the minors by Stengel, decided to do all of his pitching from the set position without a windup. Using his no-windup style, Larsen pitched four-hitters in each of his four starts during September to finish with an 11—5 record.

But the stellar Yankee in the eyes of the press and most of the public was Mantle. He had finally reached the plateau so long predicted for him by Stengel. He became the ninth man in the history of baseball to win the triple crown, leading the American League in homers, runs batted in, and batting in 1956. He clouted fifty-two homers, drove in 130 runs, and hit .353. Berra slipped below .300 in the final weeks of the season to .298, but he supported Mantle with thirty homers and 105 runs batted in. Bauer, though his average of .241 was the lowest of his eight-year career in the majors, hit twenty-six homers and had eighty-four runs batted in. Gil MacDougald hit .311 and Showron .308 with twenty-three homers and ninty runs batted in. Ford wound up with a 19—6 and his 2.47 earned-run average led the league. Former reliever Kucks was 18—9 and Sturdivant 16—8.

The pennant was Stengel's seventh in eight seasons, allowing him to match the American League record of Joe MacCarthy who also won seven in eight between 1936 and 1943.

In 1956, the World Series again matched the Yankees

LEFT HANDED SLUGGER, ROGER MARIS.

and Brooklyn and was almost a reverse replay of the previous fall. This time, the Series opened at Ebbets Field and the Dodgers won the opener on October 2, 6−3. The second game might have taken the starch out of a lesser club than Stengel's Bombers. New York scored a run in the top of the first and five more in the second. Brooklyn rallied for six in the last of the second and rolled to a 13−8 victory, giving the Dodgers a two-game edge when the action shifted to Yankee Stadium.

A huge crowd of 73,977 was on hand on October, 6 when the Yanks won, 5−3. They evened the Series the next day with a 6−2 triumph. One of the most momentous games in Series history was the fifth game of the set played on Monday, October 8. Don Larsen, his gem preserved by a sensational catch by Mantle, pitched a perfect no-hit game against Brooklyn. Mantle's homer provided the only necessary run as the Yanks won, 2−0. Pandemonium broke loose when Babe Pinelli's right arm shot up calling a third strike on pinchhitter Dale Mitchell to end the game. To Stengel, the win giving the Yanks a 3−2 lead in the Series was more important than the historical oddity. On October 9, the dazed Dodgers hung on with a 1−0 victory in ten innings to force a seventh game for the second straight year. But the Bombers began unloading the long ball early and often, coasting to a 9−0 win in the clinching contest.

Stengel had now won six World Series titles in seven tries during his eight years as Yankee manager.

As the opening of the 1957 season drew near, Stengel had on his hands a team that had set an American League record of 190 homers the previous season and was returning almost completely intact.

Weiss, however, was not inactive. Mickey McDermott, one of the prime disappointments of the previous season on the mound, was dispatched to the Kansas City A's. Along with him went pitcher Tom Morgan, the third stellar rookie of the 1951 crop that included Mantle, MacDougald, Noren, former Oriole Billy Hunter, and Jack Urban, a Minor League prospect. In return, the Yankees obtained pitcher Art Ditmar, former most valuable player pitcher Bobby Shantz, and Minor League infield Clete

Boyer. The first of a series of trades between the Yankees and the A's, the deal was to have many significant benefits for the Yanks.

To this aggregation was also added the harvest of an outstanding rookie crop from the Yankee farm system. Included in the men who remained with the club after spring training were Bobby Richardson, Tony Kubek, Woodie Held, and Ralph Terry. All were to play key roles in the remaining years of the Stengel era at Yankee Stadium and were to serve as the mainstays of the Ralph Houk period as well. However, they were to represent the last great graduating class from the once-proud farm teams. Changing Yankee management, and new baseball laws aimed almost entirely at the Yankees and Dodgers, were to cripple the magnificent Minor League operation that had fed the Yankees.

Whitey Ford again opened the season for the Yankees and turned in his usual workmanlike job, defeating Washington, 2 – 1.

However, Ford's arm began to trouble him shortly. In fact, his problems began with his very next start, also against the Senators, although he easily won the game. After struggling through two more starts, Ford was told that he had tendonitis in his left shoulder. The prescribed cure was rest and relaxation.

Despite the absence of Ford on a regular basis, the Yankees ripped off a six-game winning streak in early May and moved into first place. On May 7, they rolled into Cleveland for a two-game series that started with a night game matching Sturdivant against flame-throwing lefty Herb Score of the Indians. In the first inning, MacDougald smacked a line drive back through the middle, which hit Score in the face, knocking him into semi-conciousness. Score was carried from the field and never regained his stature as one of the most promising of American League pitchers. MacDougald, likewise was affected by the incident, never showing himself to be the hitter he had been before the tragedy.

It was an off-the-field event that made most of the early-season headlines in 1957, however. Although later celebrated as "the Copacabana incident," the evening was really a birthday party for Billy Martin, involving an entire evening of travels around well-known New York spots. Dinner was at Danny's Hide-A-Way a famous steak restaurant. Then came the show given by popular recording star Johnny Ray at the Empire Room of the Waldorf Astoria. Then the group, which included Hank Bauer, Yogi Berra, Mickey Mantle, Whitey Ford, Johnny Kucks and all their wives, and guest-of-honor bachelor Billy Martin, moved on to the Copacabana where Sammy Davis, Jr. was performing.

What happened thereafter became the subject of many articles and reports in the press, which may have been somewhat at variance with the facts. During Davis' performance, one member of a group of less-than-sober bowlers yelled a racial epithet at Davis, who stopped his show to speak to the man. Bauer told the drunk in no uncertain terms to keep quiet. An argument developed. At this point, several divergent versions of the story were presented. The drunk claimed Bauer assaulted him in the men's room. Bauer steadfastly denied hitting anybody. A later report before a grand jury indicated that two Copa bouncers actually beat up the drunk.

At any rate, Weiss blamed Martin for the ugly publicity from the incident. The press had a field day. The drunk sued Bauer for $1 million. The grand jury dismissed the case against all of the Yankees and the matter was largely forgotten by everybody except the Yankee management. Topping fined all present $1,000 (save young Kucks who got off with a $500 levy) and Weiss, who had long been seeking an excuse, traded Martin.

Stengel was heartbroken when he lost Martin, although the developments in the Yankee infield had actually made him expendable anyhow. When Carey sprained his ankle early in the season, Martin was shifted to third and Richardson moved in at second. When Carey returned, Martin was benched because Richardson's steady play and strong hitting earned him the second-base job.

Meanwhile, the Yankees began to stumble along at a .500 pace and shortly the White Sox were a half-dozen games ahead of them, snuggly settled into first place. A wild melee at Comiskey Park between the two teams in early June ignited a nine-game Yankee winning streak.

Star Chicago outfielder Larry Doby was knocked down by an Art Ditmar pitch and exchanged words with the pitcher. A fight ensued involving most players on both clubs including, naturally, Stengel. Doby, Walt Dropo of Chicago, and Billy Martin were thrown out of the game. But the Yanks won the game, and the White Sox were on the way down and were never a factor in the race thereafter.

One of the crucial parts of the Yankee machine during the drive toward the 1957 pennant was pitcher Bobby Shantz. Hardly an unknown in baseball, Shantz had been selected as the Most Valuable Player in the American League, one of the few pitchers so honored, for his somewhat prodigious feat of winning twenty-four games for the Philadelphia A's in 1952, a club that finished fourth largely on the strength of his left arm. But that left arm also was subject to a series of freak accidents and injuries over the next four years and these rendered Shantz almost totally ineffective. He was, therefore, a minor throwin on the deal that brought Art Ditmar to New York.

But once in a Yankee pinstripe jersey, Shantz revived. In 1957, Ford's arm ailments and a disappointing season for Kucks placed Shantz in the starting rotation. He finished the year 11−5 and led the league with a 2.45 earned-run average. Particularly in the early going, Shantz played a pivotal role. Ford finally returned late in the season and also pitched enough to compile an 11−5 record.

Despite the problems of injuries, the Yankees rolled along. They even survived an injury to Mantle, clearly the key man in their entire arsenal.

In mid-August, Mantle suffered shin splints that sent the powerful slugger to the sidelines intermittently for the remainder of the season and cost him a chance at the Triple Crown for the second straight year. As it was, he finished with thirty-four homers, a .365 batting average and ninety-four runs batted in, and he was named the American League's Most Valuable Player for the second straight year. He was hospitalized at Weiss' insistence during early September. After his release, Mantle led the Yanks on a charge in which they won seven of eight games. On September 21, they beat Boston while Kansas City was eliminating Chicago, giving New York its third pennant in a row. Meanwhile, the Braves, now playing in Milwaukee after moving from Boston in 1953, won their first National League pennant in the Wisconsin city to set up the first Yankee — Braves World Series ever.

At the time much was made of the fact that more than half of the men on the Kansas City roster were former Yankees or one-time Yank farmhands. What was often overlooked was that many of the outstanding players in baseball had been developed in the Yankee Minor League system and many, including Bill Virdon, were later to come back to haunt the club. One such instance presented itself in the 1957 Series.

The Series got underway on October 2 at Yankee Stadium with a 3—1 Yankee win. Lew Burdette, a former Yankee farmhand, pitched the Braves to a 4—2 win the next day to square the Series, and both clubs took off for Milwaukee's County Stadium. The first two Series games ever played in Milwaukee were split, the Yanks winning 12—3, and losing 7—5. Burdette pitched the crucial fifth game and fired a sterling 1—0 shutout win to give the Braves a one-game edge as the Series shifted back to New York.

Once again, matters became deadlocked on October 9 when the Bombers took the sixth game, 3—2, to force a seven-game Series for the third year in succession. Pitching with only two days rest, Burdette came back for the decisive seventh and turned in another shutout, winning this one 5—0, to give Milwaukee its first Series championship.

The Series ending was something of an anticlimax to what had been an unusual year for the Yankees. Largely as a result of their overwhelming talent, deep bench, and sharp managing by Stengel, they had won another pennant. Mantle was the Most Valuable Player and deservedly so, but he hit eighteen homers less than in the previous year; Berra batted only .251 with twenty-four homers and managed eighty-two runs batted in, despite a slump that lasted almost half of the season. Ford pitched only 129 innings as contrasted with the 226 of 1956, but the Yankees did win the pennant. After the seven-game struggle in the

CASEY STENGEL IN HIS LAST DAYS AS A YANKEE SKIPPER.

World Series, the Braves had several uncomplimentary remarks to make about the Yanks. One was that they would
not finish fifth in the National League. Burdette was
quoted as saying that he would love to face the Yanks again
in 1958 since he was sure the Braves would win their pennant "but I'm not so sure about them."

Stengel, one of the most competitive men in the history
of baseball, said uncharacteristically little but he seethed
much. He had won eight flags in nine years as Yankee
manager, but now he had another goal—to meet and beat
Milwaukee in the 1958 Series.

Stung by the Braves remarks and Stengel's prodding,
the Yanks literally burst out of the starting gate when the
1958 season opened and they roared away from the pack
even faster than usual. After winning seven of their first
eight games, they started a ten-game winning streak on May
13, which was not stopped until May 24 when nemesis
Frank Lary beat them, 3−2, at Detroit.

After a Sunday doubleheader sweep at Cleveland on
May 25, the astonishing Yankee record stood at 25−6. In
the first thirty-one games, the pitching staff hung up nine
shutouts and hurled eight games in which they allowed just
one run. Bob Turley was the bellweather. Exhibiting a live
fastball and super breaking stuff, Turley threw seven complete games in seven starts including four shutouts, allowing only seven runs and thirty-one hits in sixty-three innings. However, on May 27, Turley was shelled out inside
of five innings at Kansas City and was charged with a 7−3
defeat.

The setback was a temporary one for Turley as he
went on to his best all-around season, winning twenty-one
and losing seven with a 2.98 earned-run average. He was
the only twenty-game winner in the American League that
season. Turley won his tenth game on June 11.

By August 3, the Yankees were seventeen games
ahead of the second-place Indians, and sportwriters were
predicting that the Yankees would clinch the pennant by
the end of the month. Even more awesome, every other
team in the league was playing under .500 ball, Cleveland
having the second best record in the circuit at fifty-one
wins and fifty-two defeats. But on that afternoon, the

Yankees lost both ends of a doubleheader to Chicago. Dick
Donovan beat them, 3−1, on a three-hitter in the opener,
and Ray Moore won the nighcap, 4−0, with a five-hitter. In
the next seventeen days, the Yankees chopped six and a
half games off their lead.

Stengel was infuriated. Normally, he restrained
himself during a losing streak, preferring to hold his
criticism until the team started winning. But on August 18,
Stengel ordered a team workout on an off-day at Yankee
Stadium. The next night, the Yanks lost to Cleveland, suffering their ninth loss in twelve games. It was their worst
streak in five years. Finally, on August 20, Art Ditmar defeated the Indians, 7−1.

The Ditmar win straightened out the Yankees long
enough for them to complete their run to the pennant. The
clinching came at Kansas City on September 14 when Duke
Maas won the first game of a doubleheader, 5−3.

Although they once again won a pennant, their fourth
in a row and Stengel's ninth, matching Connie Mack's
American League record, they played poorly the final two
months of the season. In August, the Yankees were 15−16
and in September 12−12, putting them one game under
.500 for the final two months of the campaign. One of the
prime reasons for this slump was that Ford suffered elbow
troubles. After beating Boston, 2−0, on August 8 for his
seventh shutout and fourteenth win, Ford went to the
sidelines and did not win another game all season. Larsen
also suffered an elbow injury at almost the same time. With
his pitching thinned out, Stengel struggled to maintain the
team's momentum. Pitching built the enormous early lead,
but defense and offense had to protect enough of it to win
the flag. Stengel well knew that baseball is a pitching game,
but he had to win without it. He did.

When he did pitch, Ford was superb. His earned-run
mark of 2.01 led the American League for the second time
in three seasons. Overall, the Yankee pitching staff paced
the circuit with a team earned-run average of 3.22.

In the bullpen, the sagging Bob Grim was supplanted
by one of the sensational relievers in Yankee history—
Ryne Duren. Duren rated with Johnny Murphy, Grim, and
Luis Arroyo. His act of unloading a wild heave onto the

screen for his first warmup was a physche job that made a very strong impression on opposing hitters. His thick glasses made a strong mark as well, but it was his blazing fastball that retired the batters.

Mantle was again the leader of the Yankees in the field and won his third home-run crown with forty-two while batting .304 and driving in ninety-seven runs. Howard raised his average to .314 as a more-or-less regular in the outfield and behind the plate, hit eleven homers and drove in sixty-six, while Berra hit .266 with twenty-two homers and ninety runs batted in. Norm Siebern, the rookie left-fielder was the Yanks' third .300 hitter, making the plateau right on the button. Stengel purposely held him out of the last game of the year to protect his .300 average.

Stengel was able to achieve his wish when Milwaukee won its second National League pennant and earned the right to meet the Bombers in the 1958 Series. But the Series did not begin with any promise of revenge for the previous year's loss. Opening at Milwaukee on October 1, the Braves got the first game, 4−3, in 10 innings, and the second, 13−5. Larsen got the Yanks into the win column on October 4 by winning game three at Yankee Stadium, 4−0, but Spahn gave the Braves a seemingly-insurmountable three-games-to-one edge by taking the Sunday game, 3−0.

But then the Yankees began one of the most startling turnarounds in Series history. Only the 1925 Pirates had been able to win a Series after trailing, three games to one, and, as one writer put it, "they were playing the Washington Senators."

History or no, the Yankees came to life in game five, socking the Braves, 7−0, before heading back to Milwaukee still one game from extinction. On October 8 at County Stadium, New York stayed alive with a wild, 4−3, ten-inning victory in which Stengel used four pitchers. Thus, the Yanks faced a seventh game in the Series for the fourth time in four years. They had lost two of the preceding three, but they were not to lose this one. Perhaps still smarting under the sting of the Braves' commentary after the 1957 defeat, the Yanks won, 6−2, behind the combined pitching of Larsen and Turley. Revenge was now Stengel's;

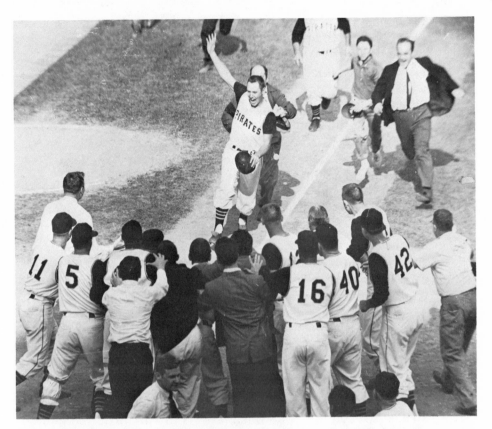

**STENGEL'S LAST WORLD SERIES ENDED WITH PIRATES SECOND
BASEMAN BILL MAZEROSKI'S HOMER IN 1960.**

THE OLD YANKEE STADIUM . . . THE HOUSE THAT RUTH BUILT.

the hard feelings engendered in Milwaukee the year before by a Stengel remark about "bush" fans was now followed by the broad grin of victory.

As satisfying as the 1958 Series victory over Milwaukee was, it was in no way comparable to the depths of despair Stengel experienced in 1959. During his entire tenure with the Yankees, no single season came even remotely close to the disaster of 1959 for slumps, losing streaks, illness, injury, and general unhappiness. The team started poorly, got worse, and was lucky to finish third. The Yankees spent part of the early season floundering in the basement of the eight-team league, a fact that made sports page headlines across America and front page headlines in some other American League cities. The final standings showed the Yankees at 79—75, a scant four games over the break-even point.

Mantle endured merciless booing both at home and on the road throughout the season. In typical fashion, the Yankee fans blamed their superstar for the failure of the club to play well. Stengel, too, came in for his share of the beating.

In the front office, Topping, Webb, and Weiss began to secondguess the manager privately and, then, publicly. Stengel's reaction to published reports of frontoffice comment was distinctly negative. A gap began to grow between Weiss and Stengel, who had originally been inseparable. Stengel, always more than a social drinker, began to hit the bottle hard and his nights became longer and longer. He even occasionally dozed off on the bench. What he missed would not have justified watching, anyhow, as it turned out. The Yankees were horrible. Perhaps suffering from overconfidence, the club had grown old in some key spots, and also complacent. The pitching collapsed.

Compounding all of this was a series of crushing injuries. Hector Lopez, acquired from Kansas City after the season started, was hit in the elbow by a pitch and went to the bench. Mantle injured his ankle, Bill Skowron popped his back. MacDougald and Kubek collided chasing a pop fly; Kubek incurred a concussion and MacDougald suffered dizzy spells. The same week that Kubek and Mac-

Doutald smashed into each other, Andy Carey contracted hepatitis and was lost for the season.

After the 1959 season ended, the Yankees had the uncommon opportunity to watch the Los Angeles Dodgers face the Chicago White Sox in the World Series. The following spring, most sportswriters were predicting a replay for 1960, but neither the Dodgers or the White Sox made it to the Series.

The winter of 1959—1960 was one of discontent in the Yankees' Fifth Avenue offices. Topping and Webb considered firing Stengel, who was going on seventy, despite the remaining year on his contract.

Wisely, they decided against it. Having been out of the trade market entirely the previous year, Weiss was determined not to make the same mistake two years running. Before the 1960 spring training began, he engineered another deal with Kansas City that sent the aging Hank Bauer, Norm Siebern, Marv Throneberry, and Don Larsen to the A's. In exchange, the Yanks got journeyman infielder Joe DeMaestri, reserve first baseman Kent Hadley, and the only man they were really interested in, outfielder Roger Maris.

A winter's rest for the aching injuries and the presence of Maris in right field gave an entirely different cast to the entire Yankee situation. The debacle of 1959 was to become a fast-fading memory, one Stengel was happy to shove into the deepest recesses of his crowded mind.

The beginning of the season was not a real augury of things to come. Although he refused to concede the point, age was beginning to make slight inroads into Stengel's remarkable constitution. In late May, he was confined to a hospital suffering from a high fever and the effects of a virus. But, upon his return, the Yankees started to move and spent the entire summer engaged in a ding-dong battle with a bunch of kids from Baltimore tagged by the press, the "Baby Birds," but officially known as the Orioles. In mid-August, Mantle won a crucial game against the O's with a pair of two-run homers as Ditmar chalked up his fifth straight win, 4−3.

With fifteen games left on the schedule in September,

the Yanks held onto a miniscule .002 lead. But with Mantle, Maris, Showron, Howard, Berra, subcatcher Johnny Blanchard, and veteran utilityman Dale Long slamming balls all over the park, the Yanks streaked through the final fifteen games without a loss and won the flag by eight games.

Mantle won his fourth home-run title with forty and led the league in runs scored with 119. Maris hit thirty-nine homers and was the American League runs-batted-in leader with 112 and in slugging percentage at .581. Their slugging set the stage for Stengel's last World Series and, in most ways, the most bizarre he was ever involved in.

Surprisingly, the Pittsburgh Pirates won the National League flag for the first time since 1927. When they faced the fabled "Murderer's Row" Yankees and were crushed in four games. Much the same fate was predicted for the 1960 Pirates. The Yankees did indeed wallop the ball against Pittsburgh pitching and set a couple of dozen records for Series batting. But they did not win the title.

The Pirates won the opener at Forbes Field, 6−4, on October 5, but the Yanks bombed Pittsburgh, 16−3, in game two, and the general feeling amongst fans and writers was that the opening game was a fluke. This feeling was re-inforced at Yankee Stadium on October 8 when Ford de-lighted a crowd of 70,001 with a 10−0 shutout which in-cluded a grand slam homer by Bobby Richardson. But the key play of the entire Series may have come in the seventh inning of game four. The Yanks, trailing 3−1, had the tying runs on the bases when ElRoy Face relieved starter Vernon Law. Bob Cerv's enormous drive to the center field wall was caught in a circus catch by Bill Virdon, a former Yankee Minor League prospect, and one run scored after the catch. But the back of the rally was broken and the Pirates won, 3−2, to even the Series. Pittsburgh won the game five, 5−2, and the Yankees unleashed another rout, 12−0, at Pittsburgh in game six.

For the fifth straight time, the Yankees were engaged in a seven-game World Series. They needed a ninth-inning rally that included some brilliant base running by Mantle to tie the game after another ex-Yank prospect Hal Smith had hit a three-run homer for the Pirates. In the home ninth,

Ralph Terry was in on relief when Bill Mazeroski led off with a homer over the left field wall. Pittsburgh won the game, 10 − 9, and the Series.

Five days later at New York's Savoy Hilton Hotel, a press conference was held to announce Stengel's retirement at age seventy. Age was given as the reason and Stengel later said, "I'll never make the mistake of being seventy again." Actually, Topping and Webb had groomed Ralph Houk for the manager's job, as a backup for Stengel, and they feared Houk would leave the organization if he did not get a shot at the job. But Stengel was hardly appreciative of the reasons, whatever they were. After reading a statement prepared by the Yankee lawyers, he was asked if he really retired. "Hell, no, I was fired," he retorted. The press conference was thrown into chaos. But Houk did get the job and Stengel was finishsdth the Yankees.

But he was far from finished in baseball, as the Yankee owners were to ruefully learn in less than two years.

CHAPTER 8

Casey's Clowns

The following year 1961, was a bad year for Casey Stengel. Actually, any year Stengel was not in baseball was a bad year. He spent most of his time in his bank in North Hollywood, California. On September 29, 1961 he accepted George Weiss' offer to become the first manager of the new National League team in New York.

"I'm happy to be asked to run the New York Knickerbockers," said Stengel, not even hep to the new name of the Metropolitan Baseball Club or the Mets.

Weiss himself was retired by the Yankees a few days after Stengel had been let go for not winning the 1960 World Series. He had nothing to do but roam around his Greenwich, Connecticut, home with his wife Hazel who griped, "I married George for better or worse, but not for lunch. He has to get a job."

The formation of the Mets was a desperate measure by organized baseball to prevent the formation by Branch Rickey of a third Major League. Rickey had set up the Continental Baseball League, whose main goal was to bring National League baseball back to New York. Gotham had been abandoned by the National League when the Giants and Dodgers left the Big Apple for San Francisco and Los Angeles after the 1957 season. Many New Yorkers sorely missed the National League and some even made quiet trips to Philadelphia to watch their former heroes play the Phillies.

Those same folks did not rush up to Yankee Stadium to watch the Stengel-led Yankees in 1958−1959 and 1960. Those were the days when rooting for the Yankees was "like rooting for U.S. Steel."

William A. Shea was the focal point of Mayor Robert Wagner's committee to bring the National League back. The Continental League was to include New York, Toronto, Buffalo, Houston, Denver, Atlanta, Dallas-Fort Worth, Minneapolis-St. Paul, and San Diego. It never got off the ground, but is was alive for a little over a year, and it forced the majors to act.

Rickey, the eighty-year-old president of the Continental League and the father of baseball's farm system, stormed Congress with anti-trust legislation in an effort to get the Continental League off the ground. The decision was made in August 1960 when the two majors decided to expand to ten clubs each from the traditional eight. The American League beat the National League by a year, going full speed ahead in 1960. The National League decided to wait until 1962, but included New York and Houston in their plans. Now the Continental League could be disbanded. It had served its purpose.

Mrs. Charles Shipman Payson (formerly Joan Whitney) was the principal backer of the New York Continental League team. When the National League included New York in its expansion plans, she stepped to the forefront and asked to buy the new club. Co-backers included Dwight Davis, Jr., G. Hebert Walker, Jr., William Simpson, and M. Donald Grant.

Grant eventually became Mrs. Payson's minister of finace and overseer of the ball club operation. Both Grant and Mrs. Payson were long-time New York Giants fans. They had sought to keep the Giants in New York by buying them from Horace Stoneham before he moved West, but to no avail. Grant, from Montreal originally, and a senior partner in the Wall Street brokerage house Fahnestock & Co., now needed a baseball man to run Mrs. Payson's new toy.

He turned to Weiss, instead of Charles Hurth, the former president of the Southern League who had been recommended by Rickey. Weiss became the Mets' new president, with Grant the chairman of the board.

Mrs. Joan Shipman Payson, one of the world's wealthiest women, now owned the Mets. Weiss had no ballpark, no players, and no manager. The price for the Mets was $1.8 million. By 1969, after they had won the pennant and World Series, they were worth $12 million. Mrs. Payson did not make a bad deal, but at the beginning it looked like the other National League owners had taken advantage of the poor lady.

**ONE OF CASEY'S AMAZIN' METS DURING 1962, SECOND BASEMAN
HOT ROD KANEHL.**

Weiss hired Stengel in late September 1961 as his manager for 1962 but Casey did not even show up for the expansion draft in Cincinnati. It was to take place in the city in which the World Series had ended, and Stengel guessed the Yankees would need more than five games to win over the Reds. He was wrong; the Yanks won it in five and precluded a return to New York. Thus, Stengel was in New York when the expansion draft took place in Cincinnati. It did not really matter, as Weiss had hired "Fordham" Johnny Murphy as his New England scout and administrative assistant. Murphy scouted the National League to see what might be available.

What was available was terrible. Paul Richards, the head man at Houston said, "We have been bleeped."

In the expansion draft, Houston and New York were to take two players apiece at $75,000 from each of the eight teams; then, if they wanted to, another at $50,000 with a final total of four as maximum who were designated as premium players at $125,000.

The Mets picked Gil Hodges, the tired old first baseman from the Los Angeles Dodgers; Elio Chacon, and infielder of dubious ability from the Reds; Hobie Landrith, Giant catcher from the unlikely town of Strawberry Plains, Tennessee; Don Zimmer, the oft-beaned third baseman then with the Cubs; Joe Christopher, an outfielder with the Pirates; Felix Mantilla, an infielder without much desire from the Braves; Lee Walls, a bespectacled outfielder from the Phillies; Gus Bell, another over-the-hill outfielder from the Reds; Ed Bouchee, a first baseman with a tainted morals record from the Phillies; pitcher Jay Hook, an engineer by trade, from the Reds; Roger Craig, who was to become known as Losing Pitcher Craig, from the Dodgers; Ray Daviault of the Giants; and Al Jackson, Bob Miller, and Craig Anderson, all from the Cardinals.

Weiss filled his roster by sending Walls and $125,000 to the Dodgers for second baseman Charlie Neal, the hero of the 1959 World Series. He bought Frank Thomas, a sometimes-slugging outfielder from the Braves; Richie Ashburn, a one time great with the phillies in centerfield, but now over-the-hill with the Cubs; and pitchers Clem Labine, Billy Loes, and Johnny Antonelli, all former New

York or Brooklyn heroes. He added outfielders Jim Hickman, Bobby Gene Smith, and John DeMerit, plus catchers Myron Joe Ginsberg and "Choo Choo" Coleman.

In the front office, author and raconteur Tom Meany was named public relations director, with Lou Niss made the traveling secretary. Wid Mathews headed the western scouting setup, with thirty-six bird dogs under the direction of Bill Bergesch.

Stengel and Weiss named as their coaches Red Kress, a former Giants coach and pitcher; Solly Hemus, former Cardinals manager; Cookie Lavegetto, who had broken Bill Bevens' 1946 World Series no hitter, and Red Ruffing, the former Yankee pitching great. Gus Mauch, former Yankee trainer under Stengel, was named to heal and patch the fledgling Metsies.

The Houston team had drafted mainly young, untried players, but New York went for aging, big-name players who might prove useful for a year or two, and who could be expected to bring National League fans back to the Polo Grounds, which was to be the Mets temporary home.

Ironically two of the Houston Colt 45s best youths became later-day Met stars: catcher Jerry Grote and outfielder Rusty Staub, both acquired through trades later, with Staub coming to the Mets via Montreal.

Weiss negotiated what might have been the best television package ever, with the TV-radio rights going to the Liebman Bros. and to a cigarette company, Brown & Williamson. Liebman paid over $6 million for the TV rights to 126 games a year.

Right after that the shrewd former Yankee boss signed Bill Boylan to handle the press lounge at Shea Stadium. It was a popular move. Boylan had been a Minor League pitcher in the old New York Penn League. He then retired and became a Brooklyn mailman. Boylan used to rush to finish his route early, so he could park his truck outside Ebbets Field. He then would enter, put on his Dodger uniform, which he prized, and pitch batting practice for the Superbas. He knew everybody and was well liked.

Although Weiss didn't understand the mystique of the Mets as well as Stengel did, he understood that the Yankees had not really cultivated the old Dodger fans who had moved to Long Island in the general exodus to the suburbs. But George did understand that these people had been weaned on the National League, so he hired Jim Murray, a former Yankee farmhand and Betty King to cultivate groups from the island.

Making the deal with the city for the use of the Polo Grounds was not that hard, but it did require the halting of condemnation proceedings, which were underway preparatory to turning the Giants ballpark into a housing project. And the San Francisco Giants still owned the lights and certain fixtures, and they had to co-operate, and be compensated. In all, the Mets spend over $300,000 fixing up the Polo Grounds, erecting a new scoreboard, and re-sodding the field. It was to be their home until the new ball park in Flushing was complete.

As spring training started in 1962, Weiss picked St. Petersburg, Florida as his base, returning to old friends and associates. And he and Stengel accomplished in a twinkling what the Yankees had not been able to do in thirty years in St. Pete; they integrated the town. The Yankees had moved out of St. Petersburg, for a better deal in Fort Lauderdale. Both the Mets and their neighbors, the St. Louis Cardinals, found accommodations that would take care of their black players, the Mets at a place on the Gulf of Mexico and the Cards in a motel on the Causeway.

In an example of reverse pulic relations, the stiff-backed Weiss insisted that the Mets headquarters remain in the Soreno Hotel, which refused blacks. It had been his home in Yankee Spring training days. Meany, the public relations man, was also an interesting man, who knew how to entertain, but was not interested in helping out the press. It was all left to Stengel to take over the public relations of the infant club.

When the Mets arrived in St. Petersburg, a banner stretched across the main street, proclaiming, WELCOME NEW YORK METS AND CASEY STENGEL. At the Mets' motel a sign proudly stated; STENGELESE SPOKEN HERE.

In a retirement town such as St. Pete, the accomplishments of the seventy-one year-old Stengel took on an extra glow for the elderly. Everyone became a Met fan over-

ONE OF THE ORIGINAL METS,
JIM HICKMAN.

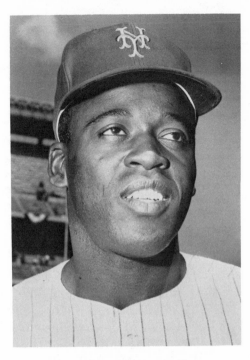

CATCHER, CHOO CHOO COLEMAN.

PITCHER GALEN CISCO.

THE MARVELOUS ONE, MARV
THRONEBERRY.

night. And the media, who had feared boredom covering a bunch of has-beens, suddenly were captivated by a seemingly rejuvenated Stengel.

"It's true I used to fall asleep on the Yankee bench," admitted Casey. "We were so efficient it put me to sleep."

At the end of one day of training, Stengel posed for pictures with Mrs. Payson and said, "Why should I be old fashioned just because I'm old?"

Hope was springing eternal for National League fans— and Casey fed that hope. All sorts of people showed up in that first training camp. There was a pitcher from Astoria named John Pappas. who could not throw; a third baseman named Dawes Hamilt, with legs like the pillars of a Roman coliseum; Bruce Fitzpatrick, another heavy-legged phenomenon whom Stengel kept talking about; and Butterball Botz, a pitcher who was perhaps the worst ever to wear a Major League uniform, even in training.

The Mets lost their first exhibition game to the Cardinals, 8−0, with only Frank Thomas' long "foul" homer giving any hope.

Casey winked and said, "It was a homer in the Polo Grounds. Would have reached the short left field wall before it curved foul."

Choo Choo Coleman hit the first Met home run, and it helped get them their first win, March 12, 1962 against the Cards, 4−3. After losing seven more in a row, the Mets beat the Tigers, 1−0, on a wind-blown triple by Gus Bell. Ray Daviault, Herb Moford, and Bob Moorhead combined for this feat. But the big battle with the new blood rivals, the New York Yankees was still to come.

On March 23, 1962 the Mets and Yankees met for the first time. Weiss had promised the Yankees he would not take another general manager job, so the Yanks were unhappy with his new position with the Mets. Stengel had been fired by the Yanks and he hated them.

It was to be the first miracle of the Metsies. They beat the Yanks, 4−3, after blowing a 3−2 lead in the ninth inning. Joe Christopher tripled in the ninth and Richie Ashburn pinch hit a single for the winning run. Roger Craig had held the Yanks for six innings to only two runs. The Yanks were trying, using Bill Stafford and Ralph Terry.

Stengel, with a Chesire cat grin, walked into the press room after the game and said, "It shows you how easy this business is."

When the Mets played the Yankees again, this time at Ft. Lauderdale, the Yankees were losing, 2 − 1, going into the eighth, but they got lucky and pulled out when a doubleplay grounder hit at Felix Mantilla hopped over his head. Moose Skowron won it with a sacrifice fly in the ninth.

Ralph Houk's Stengel successor as the Yankee manager, growled, "I had to win. I didn't want you bleeps to put us on the front pages again."

At the end of spring training Craig had pitched thirty-five innings with a neat 2.50 earned-run average. Stengel called him "the real perdotious quotient of the qualifications."

But underneath he knew that Roger's curve could bother hitters in the spring, but it might not last all season long.

The Mets wound up with a 13 − 15 record that spring, with Craig and Al Jackson as their best pitchers. Hot Rod Kanehl, hitting in luck was a .440 hitter, including one accidental pinch hit that beat the Dodgers.

Stengels' opening lineup for the Mets first game in St. Louis was: Ashburn, center field; Mantilla, shortstop; Neal, second base; Thomas, first base; Bell, right field; Hodges, first base; Zimmer, third base; Landrith, catcher; Craig, pitcher.

On the way to Sportsmans Park in the Mound City, the elevator in the lobby of the Chase Hotel in St. Louis became stuck. Sixteen Mets were in it for a full twenty minutes.

Craig said, "The first time in my life I'm the opening day pitcher, and I get stuck in an elevator. We'll be here for twenty-four hours."

It turned out to be twenty minutes.

The Mets were rained out of their first game, but opened the next night. They lost, 11 − 4. Later when a reporter asked Stengel if he was going to pray for better luck, he said, "Prayers don't win for you. You've got to do it yourself."

Landrith had three bases stolen on him without even coming close to getting anyone. Gil Hodges hit the Mets first home run, and Charlie Neal hit another, but there were many bad plays.

The Mets opened at the Polo Grounds on Friday, April 13, losing to the Pirates, 4−3. Mayor Robert Wagner showed up and was booed by fans who still blamed him for not stopping the Giants and Dodgers from leaving New York. The Mets almost won it, but Ray Daviault wild pitched Dick Groat home with the wining run.

The Polo Grounds was this writer's boyhood hang out, a large wooden structure with a fortune wasted in ob-structed views, but with an intimate view of the field and a familarity with the action not seen in Shea Stadium, Yankee Stadium, or bigger and newer concrete mausoleums like Dodger Stadium, Three Rivers Stadium, or Riverfront Stadium. It ranked with Ebbets Field and Fenway Park as a quaint part of America. Sportsmans Park in St. Louis had the same feeling and so did the old Baker Bowl in Philadelphia.

The rectangular shape of the Polo Grounds made it dif-ferent from other ballparks. It was only 257 feet down the right-field line and 297 down the left-field stripe. Center field was 483 feet away, although the sign at the center field monument between the two left- and right-field bleacher sections read 505 feet.

Bobby Thomson hit his famous home run into the lower stands, an unusual feat. It crashed into Section 33 with Andy Pafko back at the wall watching. Dusty Rhodes beat the Cleveland Indians with a pair of so-called Chinese home runs into the right-field stands, the first one breaking Bob Lemon's heart in the Series opener of 1954.

In my boyhood, Mel Ott, the stocky right fielder with number 4 on his bat, would cock his leg and thump home runs into the right-field stands. Sal Maglie, Larry Jansen, Jim Hearn, and Manager Leo Durocher, with help from Ed-die Stanky and Alvin Dark, fashioned the Little Miracle of Coogan's Bluff in 1951 when the Giants rallied from a thir-teen and a half game deficit to edge the Dodgers in the Thomson playoff. The Mets new temporary home was steeped in tradition.

Only 21,000 watched the Mets first game at the Polo Grounds. Joy and sorrow were mixed. The Metsies mystique had not caught on yet, although the crowd was solidly behind the losers and chanted, "Let's Go Mets."

Stengel made a mistake when he was interviewed by the press after the game. As do most managers, he undressed while talking to the reporters, and it was discovered that his undershorts still read: "New York Yankees" with the Yankees tophat coat of arms.

The horrendous Mets lost their first nine games. Stengel called off one game with Houston when he alone detected a raindrop.

"Can't lose today," said Craig, who was beginning to drop into the box scores as Losing Pitcher Craig.

Roger eventually lost forty-six games in two seasons, but he was a good pitcher, and he gave the Mets a chance every time he pitched. "I never ever got used to losing," said Roger.

The Mets finally won their first game in Pittsburgh on April 23, 1962. Jay Hook was the pitcher in a 9 – 1 success.

"Ninety-nine more like that and we win the pennant," clowned Stengel. "I may make Hook pitch all the rest of the games."

Hook had some talent, but he always seemed to fail in crucial spots and most felt he could not brush back the hitters or get tough when it counted.

Shortly after, a mountainous catcher, Harry Chiti, came from the Cubs to the Mets for a player that was to be named later. Chiti was so bad that the Mets named him the player-to-be-announced-later and shipped him back at the end of the season.

The Mets lost 120 games that first year, and Stengel had to get used to losing again. They did a win doubleheader from Milwaukee, and they took three of four from the Braves, with former Brave Frank Thomas destroying his olt team with three homers and 8 – 18. Thomas hit thirty-five home runs, a club record, but twenty-five of them came with the bases empty. He was a dead pull hitter who loved the Polo Grounds.

Later, while finishing up his career with the Phillies,

Thomas got into a fight with Richie Allen and was given his walking papers.

The Mets mystique was starting to grow with "Marvelous Marv" Throneberry now a part of the team. Marv had been a Yankee, probably overrated, but he was still a good prospect. He was obtained from the Baltimore Orioles, which should have told the Mets something. Weiss obtained him in a straight cash deal. Marv had a lifetime average of .238 and was a poor fielder. But he became famous after starting out as the goat of Mets fans. In the beginning, he was Gil Hodges' caddy, playing when the popular former Dodger had to beg off with physical ills at age thirty-seven.

Richie Ashburn recognized Marvelous Marv's special affinity with the fans and slowly got Throneberry to understand. In the first game of a doubleheader against Chicago, Throneberry had Don Landrum in a rundown and neatly blocked him out with as good a block as thrown by Reggie McKenzie while blocking for O. J. Simpson. The trouble is, he did not have the ball. Landrum was ruled safe. The Cubs got four runs.

Throneberry went up to hit, determined to correct the problem he had caused. Two Mets were on base when he drilled a high drive between the right fielder and center field. Marv put his head down and steamed from first to second, tearing around the bad and slid into third. Ernie Banks, the Cubs first baseman called for the ball and calmly touched first base.

"Yer out," bellowed the umpire. "You didn't touch first."

When Stengel came out roaring, he was informed that Marv had not bothered to touch second, either.

It was in this doubleheader that Lou Brock of the Cubs caught one of Al Jackson's curve balls and hit it 500 feet into the right-field bleachers, only the second time this had been done in history. Joe Adcock of the Milwaukee Braves had done it in 1953, and later Henry Aaron did it. Luke Easter had done it in a Negro League game and Schoolboy Rowe, a pitcher with the Detroit Tigers had done it in batting practice before the 1934 All Star game, but the

FRANK THOMAS HIT 34 HOME
RUNS DURING THE 1962 SEASON.

FIRST BASEMAN ED KRANEPOOL
WAS UNDER CASEY'S WING WHEN
HE WAS 17.

1969 WORLD SERIES HERO, CLEON
JONES, WAS A MET ROOKIE IN
1963.

INFIELDER AL MORAN.

bleachers in the old Polo Grounds were practically inviolate.

In the ninth inning the Mets were behind, 8−7, with two on and two out. Throneberry was the hitter. You guessed it, he struck out.

One day when Stengel came to take Ray Daviault out of the game, the young man had been victimized by poor fielding behind him. He had earned about seven outs, but nothing had gone right in the infield.

"I'm doing the job," said Ray.

"Well, maybe you could strike them out. You know we can't field grounders," replied Stengel.

Marvelous Marv had a great September. One day he hit a home run that beat the Dodgers and made all three putouts in the ninth inning.

The marvelous Marv cult was now in full swing with tee-shirts, banners, and the whole bit. "He typifies the Mets," explained one fan. "Great one day and terrible the next."

Throneberry finished as the Peepul's Choice and even complained when Eddie Bouchee dropped a popup and was booed.

"What are you trying to do," griped Marv, wiping his almost bald dome, "take over my act?"

The Mets season finally ended with 40−120 in the books and losing streaks of 9, 11, 13 and 17. Almost overlooked, but never to be forgotten were the two Bob Millers, both pitchers.

"I was shocked," admitted Stengel. "It was worse than I expected."

The second year was simply more of the same. Some of the faces changed, but the Mets still were last and awful. Duke Snider, now thirty-six and slipping, was imported from Los Angeles. The gray-haired Duke was handsome in an elderly sort of way and gave dignity, if not much else, to the Mets. Ron Hunt, the Mets first genuine good ballplayer who was young, was the second baseman. The outfield had Thomas in left, Snider in center, and young Ed Kranepool, who had joined up in the later part of 1962, in right field. Although Kranepool played for the Mets in their first season, he was not a Mets original.

Chris Cannizzaro, who had helped Coleman with the catching the first year, had a severe dislocation fracture of the top joint of his hand, and Choo Choo Coleman was the catcher.

Robert G. Lance Miller had a record of $0-12$ at one point and Robert Miller was simply trying to get in enough time to qualify for his five-year Major League pension.

Before Hunt cracked the Met infield, it had Neal at third, Al Moran at short, and Larry Burright at second. The Mets even led the Citrus standings for a while with a $1-0$ win over the Yankees included.

But they opened with eight straight losses, including two straight shutouts.

Stengel noticed improvement, saying, "last year we lost nine before we won."

After the Mets beat Milwaukee $5-4$, on April 19 at the Polo Grounds, they won the next three and eight of the next twelve. The fans started to hope again and banners sprouted like mushrooms.

Marv Throneberry did not play until May 1—"May Day" it was signaled—when he got into a game in right field and promptly played a single into a double by falling down.

"I hadn't played all year and had played first base the year before," said Marv. "Suddenly this white thing is coming at me and I had to do something."

On April 24 Carlton Willey carved out the first shutout in Mets history, a $2-0$ job over the Chicago Cubs. Willey, from the Milwaukee Braves, went on to a reasonably good season with a $9-14$ record. He, Craig, and Jackson were giving the Mets a chance in some games.

Four of Wiley's wins were shutouts, the most notable being a $5-0$ job over the Cubs, on August 24, the Mets forty-first win of the season. It made the 1963 Metsies the winninest Met team in history, exceeding by one the forty wins of 1962.

In May the Mets sent Gil Hodges to Washington, where he eventually wound up as the Senators' manager, and acquired Jimmy Piersall at about the same time.

"It's a match made in heaven," said Tommy Holmes, the baseball expert from Brooklyn.

"I need another comedian like a need a hole in the

head," growled Stengel. "But maybe he can catch a fly ball in center field."

Piersall, a great fielder in his youth with the Red Sox, smote a triple in his Met debut and ran around the bases backward when he hit the one-hundredth home run of his career. But other than that, he did not do the job. Jimmy lasted eight weeks and hit .194.

Tim Harkness, who was going to solve the first base problem, didn't, but he lasted the whole season, hitting .211.

The Mets finally sent "Marvelous Marv" Throneberry to Buffalo on cutdown day in May. He took it hard. The Marvelous Marv Fan Club threatened to boycott the Polo Grounds. They didn't but they continued to wear their fan-club teeshirts. Plans were made to hire a plane and skywrite: WELCOME HOME MARV, when an if, the Mets recalled Throneberry.

When the Mets went to Buffalo for the annual exhibition with their farmhands, they saw Throneberry for the last time. They were shocked to find he did not even play first base regularly for the Bisons.

"Sometimes we win when we play Ed bouchee. When we play Throneberry, we usually lose," stated one Buffalo writer.

In the game against the Mets, Marv missed a throw in the first inning, got one base on balls, struck out twice, and grounded out weakly in the ninth with the Bisons rallying.

Another 1963 Met of note had to be Little Abner— Tracy Stallard—whose power fastball Roger Maris had hit into the right-field stands at the Yankee Stadium on the last day of the 1961 season for his sixty-first home run, the most in baseball history in a single season.

Roger Craig, 10−24 in 1962, lost, 4−3, to his old team the Dodgers in April. He was 5−22 and finally seemed to give up. All of baseball sympathized with Roger during the course of his agonizing eighteen-game personal losing streak, which did not end until he finally beat the Cubs, 7−3.

Norm Sherry had come from the Dodgers to catch for the Mets, but even he could not help Roger's luck. Six of the eighteen straight were one-run defeats. He had a 1−0

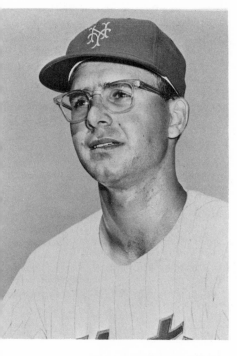

PITCHER KEN MACKENZIE.

OUTFIELDER JOHNNY LEWIS.

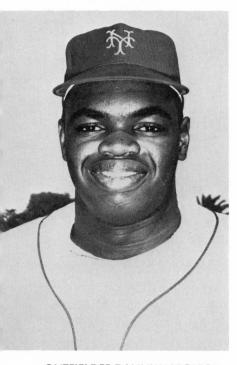

OUTFIELDER DANNY NAPOLEON.

PITCHER DENIS RIBANT.

game going into the ninth in Philadelphia, get the first one, and then made two bad pitches. Tony Gonzalez hit the first for a two-bagger, and Roy Sievers lined the other for the game-winning home run.

After his two seasons with the Mets, Craig wanted out and was traded to the Cards for outfielder George Altman and pitcher Bill Wakefield.

"No prisoner ever felt better when he was pardoned," said Roger. "My two seasons with the Mets taught me to cope with adversity."

Ken McKenzie, who joined in the first year, was a relief pitcher, the self-confessed "lowest paid member of his Yale graduating class." He thought the improvement in the Mets in 1963 was because of Al Moran at short and Ron Hunt at second.

"They make the plays and don't give too much away," said Ken.

Then there was Larry Bearnarth, a gutsy young man who did not really have the stuff to be in the bigs. Stengel loved him. Dick Lynch, just about the best pinchhitter in the majors at the time, came up to hit for Cincinnati with runners on second and third. The plan called for Bearnarth to walk Lynch by not giving him anything good to hit and keeping the ball close. Larry hit him in the kidney with the first pitch.

"Why waste time," said The Bear, "he'll remember me the next time."

Stengel liked that display of intestinal fortitude.

One of the few Mets with promise was Kranepool, the young man from James Monroe High School in the Bronx, who liked to think he could take Mel Ott's place in the hearts of New York fans. He had been signed by Bubber Jonnard, the Mets' New York scout, on the basis of nine home-run hits into the Polo Grounds right-field stands during a tryout, plus his great record with James Monroe. He hit .492 and broke Hank Greenberg's record for homers. He did not know whether he was a first baseman or a right fielder. Today the 1976 Mets still use Ed at first and in left field. He is a survivor, with thick, heavy legs, who is slow afoot, but he can hit. He helped win the 1969 pennant, went back to the minors, but returned to help in 1973 when the

Mets won again and had a big year with the bat in 1975. He is an accomplished pinchhitter and manages to stick. But he is not the great player the Mets and Stengel hoped he would be.

On June 24, 1963 at Yankee Stadium the Mets beat the Yankees in an exhibition game, 6 − 2, before a howling mob of the New Breed fans. The Yankees banned the banners waved by the Mets fans and the fat was really in the fire between the two clubs.

Mets banners in the early days read things like UP YONDER WITH GONDER (a reference to Jesse Gonder, a new catcher who didn't); and NINTH PLACE OR BUST: BLESSED ARE THE METS FOR THEY SHALL INHERIT THE PENNANT.

"Do they rehearse at night?" asked Pearsall, in wonderment one day.

The Mets lost an amazing twenty-nine of thirty-one games in 1963 at one point, during the height of losing pitcher Craig's anguish, but they did win fifty-one games, eleven more than in 1962. And they were ready to make their 1964 debut in the brand new Shea Stadium, which had been built at the pace of a slow glacier, or so it seemed.

In the ancient Polo Grounds the attendance had been good, with banners reading: LET'S GO METS. KEEP MRS. PAYSON OUT OF DEBT. There was, LET'S GO DUKE for Snider, and even a day for the grizzled, former Brooklyn Dodger, September 12. They gave Duke a night at the Polo Grounds, something he never dreamed would happen when he was the center fielder of the hated Dodgers at Ebbets Field.

"I don't know what to say," said the Duke. "I look up into the stands and it looks like Ebbets Field. You can't take the Dodgers out of Brooklyn, but the Mets are wonderful"

Snider hit fourteen homers, with a .257 batting average. He played in 129 games and lent a touch of class to the Mets. But he was through, and his thirty-six-year-old legs groaned all season. He did, however, hit his four-hundredth National League homer as a Met.

"I learned more baseball from Casey Stengel this season than in all my fifteen previous seasons in the NL," said Snider.

The Mets were doing pretty well at the box office in the Polo Grounds, staging a day for Willie Mays in May of 1963 on a Saturday. Mays drew 49,341 customers, but the Mets drew 53,880 the next day and beat the Giants, 4 – 2. In fact, when Stengel's lancers beat Alvin Dark's Giants two straight in the Polo Grounds in September, Duke was so mad he kept his team after the second game and had them practice for an hour and a half. Casey liked that.

On September 15, 1963 the Mets held their first official Banner Day with some of these in contention:

KNOW WHY THE METS ARE SUCH GOOD LOSERS? PRACTICE MAKES PERFECT. YOU MAY DOWN ON YOUR CANS, BUT YOUR FIRST WITH THE FANS. I PLEDGE ALLEGIANCE TO THE METS OF THE NATIONAL BASEBALL LEAGUE, AND TO THE POLO GROUNDS FOR WHICH IT STANDS, ONE TEAM, UNDER CASEY, INDIVISIBLE, WITH FUN AND EXCITEMENT FOR ALL.

Then the ballplayers walked out on the field and held up carefully arranged signs that spelled out: TO THE METS FANS, WE LOVE YOU TOO! Stengel carried the the exclamation point.

The Mets played their last game at the Polo Grounds on September 18, 1963, their second farewell in two years. They thought that Shea would be ready for 1963 and staged an official farewell at the end of 1962.

"It took the Giants over fifty years to bury the P. F., but the Mets did it twice in two years," growled Louie Kleppel, the rotund bleacher fan who adopted the Mets after his Giants moved to the Coast.

The Phillies beat the Mets that last day, 5 – 1, with Craig Anderson, the losing pitcher. There was a banner that foretold of the Mets future in Shea: WE SHALL OVERCOME.

The closing of the Polo Grounds was a sad day for all true baseball fans. It was a true old-time park. Many of the

Giants fans never adopted the Mets and simply came to the Polo Grounds to see the National League play. One fan, nicknamed Molotov, even took leave from his job in the post office to make an annual West Coast trip every season in June to root for the Giants in Seals Stadium and later Candlestick Park.

"I can't root for the Mets," said Lemonhead, another former Giant fan. "And Stengel still means the Yankees to me. They stink."

But at Shea, for 1964, the New Breed did indeed root for the Mets. Shea opened to a crowd of 50,132 customers and went on from there. The Mets drew 1,732,597, second only to the Los Angeles Dodgers. And they outdrew the American League champs the Yankees by a whopping 426,959, more than Stengel's old Boston Bees used to draw for the entire season.

Five times the Mets got over 50,000 in attendance, with the Dodgers doing that on six occasions, and the Yankees two. Shea also drew a sellout to the 1964 All Star game and 55,396 for the annual Mayor's Trophy game with the Yanks. Shea was helped by the Worlds Fair, which operated during both of its first two seasons and for Stengel's two years in Flushing.

The new ballpark, built on an area that had once been a garbage dump, was not far from the area made famous by the Trilon and Perisphere of the 1939 World's Fair. It was named after the attorney who had done such a good job in getting the National League back to New York, William A. Shea.

The first nine games at Shea drew 238,532, compared to the 1963 count of 1,080,108 for the entire season in the Polo Grounds.

The early games at Shea did not include visits from the Giants and Dodgers. Later when the former New York teams came into Shea, the Giants and Willie Mays drew 357,475, and the Dodgers 326,231. It was Babylon in Queens.

Although Shea is now considered to be obsolete, it was plush and modern in 1965, with carpeted spacious dressing rooms for home and visiting teams and even nice quarters for the umpires. There are four decks: field level, loge, mezzanine, and upper. But the field of action was much farther away than it was at the Polo Grounds.

The foul lines are not bad, at 341 feet to right and left fields, and 410 feet to center. Shea is a cold place in the fall as anyone who attended the night portion of the 1973 World Series will tell you. There are swirling winds in the center field area, which make Joe Willie Namath unhappy in the fall. And the drainage backs up from the nearby flushing bay, making it somewhat similar to center field in the old Polo Grounds, which always saw the Harlem River back up onto the playing field in wet weather. Unlike some of the newer ball parks, the playing surface is not Tartan turf or some other artificial surface, which changes the basic way the game is played.

The 1964 Mets had swapped Roger Craig to the Cardinals for George Altman and Bill Wakefield. Altman was not too interested and hit only .230. An occasional power hitter, he eventually went to Japan and is now the Grand Old American of Nipponese Baseball. But that did not help Stengel at Chez Stengel, otherwise known as Shea Stadium.

In June the fledgling team got shortstop Roy McMillan from for pitcher Jay Hook and cash. He was known as the human steam shovel, and he tightened the Mets defense immeasureably. They also picked up third baseman-left fielder Charlie Smith from the Chicago White Sox. He really could not field and hit only .239, but he did hit twenty homers to lead the team. Also, Frank Lary, the Detroit Tiger veteran joined up and did well for awhile.

Youngsters Cleon Jones, an outfielder, and Ed Kranepool, wound up in Buffalo for part of the year, but their promise was there. Carlton Willey, was hurt in spring training when a line drive from the bat of Gates Brown of the Tigers broke his jaw. He was out for two months, came back early, and hurt his arm. Exit Willey.

Ron Hunt, the 1963 Most Valuable Player and the best player the Mets had, was hurt with nagging injuries most of the season. He had been the National League All Star second baseman. But he hung in there. So did Stengel, who often asked the pitchers to name their catcher. Most often

1969 METS MANAGER GIL HODGES GIVES AUTOGRAPH WHILE CASEY LOOKS ON.

PITCHER DICK SELMA.

RON SWOBODA WAS GOING TO BE CASEY'S NEXT BABE RUTH.

this was Chris Cannazzaro, but then he got hurt. Hawk Taylor and Jesse Gonder saw some action too.

Frank Thomas was shipped to the Phillies late in the season. Joe Christopher proved to be the find of 1964 with his solid hitting. He earned the regular right field job when Altman got hurt and hit .300 with seventy-six runs batted in. Kranepool came back from Buffalo and played first base.

The pitching was spotty. Larry Bearnarth, the bullpen hero of the year before, came up with arm trouble. Al Jackson, Jack Fisher, Galen Cisco, and Tracy Stallard all were starters. Fisher won ten games, as did Stallard, with Cisco winning six. Wakefield, coming out of the bullpen, appeared in sixty-two games, the most on the team.

No team in the history of baseball could lose with the artistry of the Mets. Baseball's longest day began at Shea Stadium at 1:05 P.M. on Sunday, May 31, 1964, and did not end until 11:25 P.M. that night. The Mets managed to lose two games to the San Francisco Giants, 5 – 3 and 8 – 2, with the second game requiring twenty-three innings to complete. In the process 57,037 customers consumed 21,236 cans of beer, 28,915 cans of soft drinks, 12,566 hot dogs, and 6,502 bags of peanuts. And the souvenir stands did a whopping business.

The four umpires made the mistake of skipping a meal between games, which meant that Ed Sudol, Paul Proyer, Ed Secory, and Ken Burkhart were famished at the end of the night. The Mets were scheduled for an exhibition game with their Williamsport Eastern League farmteam the next night, but Stengel had it canceled. Kranepool, the teenage prodigy, had played a doubleheader with the Buffalo farmteam at Syracuse the day before. He was called up and got off the plane in New York and went right to the ballpark, playing the whole doubleheader on just a bowl of soup.

The second game marathon went seven hours and twenty-three minutes before the Giants finally won it on Del Crandall's ground ball double to right field after Jim Davenport had started at the top of the twenty-third with a triple. Cap Peterson was intentionally walked. Galen Cisco was the loser after throwing nine innings off five hit relief

THE OL' PERFESSER OF THE METS, CASEY STENGEL (Left) 1963 (Right) 1948.

pitcher. Jay Alou knocked in the extra San Francisco run.

Less than a month later on June 21, Jim Bunning of the Phillies was the superhero as he pitched a perfect game against the Metsies. Philadelphia won, 6 − 0, and Jim's wife Mary and daughter Barbara who were across the street at the World's Fair waited in vain for Jim to join them after his pitching chore. It was the first game of a doubleheader, but Bunning was kept around for such chores as Ralph Kiner's postgame show and, eventually, "The Ed Sullivan Show" that night. He got $3,000 for the latter appearance.

In the last two innings, the Mets fans were cheering for Bunning. It was the first perfect game in the majors since 1880, with the exception of Don Larsen's perfect game in the 1958 World Series.

In August of 1964 the Mets swapped Frank Lary to the Milwaukee Braves for a young pitcher, Dennis Ribant, a Canadian who had played hockey in the Detroit Red Wings system, started against Pittsburgh and was creamed for one of the longest homers in Forbes Field history by Jerry Lynch. But he came back a few days later in Shea to shutout the Pirates for his first Major League win, 5 − 0.

On July 31, 1964 Stengel reached his seventy-fourth birthday. In September of the same year, Bing Devine joined the New York team as special assistant to the aging Mets president, George Weiss. Eddie Stanky came from the Cardinals as a troubleshooter, and the team obtained southpaw great Warren Spahn.

Of course Spahn was in his dotage as a winning pitcher, being forty-three. Warren had had thirteen twenty-win National League seasons, but he was 6 − 13 with Milwaukee and fading fast. Both his knees were shot, but he still insisted he could start and win.

He was officially listed as a player-coach and was paid the princely wage of $85,000. "I'm a pitcher first and a coach after that," said Spahn. "I have 356 wins and want 400."

He never got them despite Stengel giving him every opportunity in 1964 and the first part of 1965.

The 1964 season ended with fifty-three wins, two more than the previous season. It was the third straight cellar finish for Stengel—and this time he had been on the receiving end of a perfect game, unlike the Larsen masterpiece when he had been with the Yankees. The team lost sixteen of its first nineteen games, and never really had a chance. But the legend of the Metsies as fantastic losers was growing.

In 1965 the Mets went backward, with only fifty wins and one-hundred-twelve defeats, the worst since their inception in 1962. They again finished last, the many injuries suffered by second baseman Ron Hunt contributing to this situation. First he had a finger injury, then a shoulder separation, and he was out from April 30 to August 3.

But the main casualty was Stengel himself. The Mets held their annual Oldtimers Day on July 24. That evening, Stengel had been feeling no pain, while celebrating. He fell while getting out of a taxicab. It was to be his swan song as Mets manager. Charles Dillon Stengel had broken his hip, and Wes Westrum took over as interim manager.

Some were surprised at this move, like Yogi Berra, now thirty-nine, the former Yankee great who had managed his club to the 1964 pennant, and had joined the Mets as a player-coach early in the season. He played a few games then retired to coaching, but the Mets went to Westrum.

Wes, the catcher for the 1951 Miracle Giants of Leo Durocher, had taken a calculated risk by joining the Mets for 1965. And he decided to go with kids. "It's time to give youth a chance," said Wes. "We have looked at old men for four years, but now is the time to change."

On August 30, 1965, walking falteringly with the aid of a cane, the Mets held a gloomy press conference at the Essex Hotel.

"Right now I am not capable of walking out on the ball field," said Stengel. "It's not proper for myself to limp out there." said Stengel. "If I can't run out to take a pitcher out of the box, I don't want to complete my term."

He also added, "I think the club has done exceptionally good under Westrum. When I had them, they were green as grass. Now he has competition for jobs. If a fellow gets hurt you got somebody to play and you can trade someone, too."

It was not unexpected but the baseball world was shocked to realize that Stengel would no longer be part of the everyday scene.

"I believe that I am leaving four or five players who will be here ten years or so. Ron Swoboda will be here a long time and they won't laugh at him next year with his strikeouts. He can be a big man. So can Tug McGraw, Dennis Musgraves, and Johnny Stephenson. And my old man at shortstop Roy McMillan is something special."

Casey also praised Hunt as a first division ball player—and a winner.

Stengel's record for the Mets in 1965 was 31−64, under Westrum they were 19−48.

The Yankees were on the West Coast when the news of Casey's forced retirement broke, but Whitey Ford put it perfectly, "I hope he stays in baseball. Just because he likes it so much and because he is such a great guy even though he used to get a lot of players mad at him. . . . "

CHAPTER 9

Hall of Fame

Following his formal retirement as manager of the New York Mets on August 30, 1965, many baseball observers may have felt that they had seen the last of Casey Stengel. They didn't know Casey very well. Within a year, Stengel was to be responsible for a new regulation concerning inductions into baseball's Hall of Fame, was to get elected under what might well be termed "the Stengel clause" and re-emerge with more of the millions of well-chosen words for which he was famous. Baseball, and all of the rest of the world, was to continue, much to its delight, to hear from Stengel long after his so-called retirement.

Stengel was retired by the Yankees, actually retired himself from the Mets and, in reality, never retired from baseball for a second after he became aware of its existence as a young boy.

For this, baseball was blessed.

Finally, after a half-century of education by the Ol' perfessor, baseball itself began to get into the zany act he created. A non-existent "presentation" ceremony was arranged at St. Petersburg prior to the first Mets intrasquad game on March 8, 1966, to which Stengel and Edna were invited. The presentation, something supposedly involving George Weiss, in fact turned out to be an announcement by Ford Frick of Stengel's election into the Hall of Fame.

Elaborate precautions were taken in advance to insure that Stengel was not aware of what really was to take place at Huggins-Stengel Field that day. The car in which he went to the ballpark never had its radio turned on.

Stengel's friends were afraid that a news broadcast on the radio might tip the story to Stengel.

The whole system by which Stengel was elected to the Hall of Fame was especially constructed for just that purpose. After Stengel's retirement as manager of the Mets and his appointment as a vice-president of the club, pressure began to build to elect him to the Hall. In 1955, Joe DiMaggio had been elected after having been retired for

less than five years and a rule was passed making that
length of time mandatory for any player or manager to be
elected. The rule was altered to permit immediate election
of anyone over sixty-five. Stengel was the obvious target of
this rule and a quiet mail ballot was conducted among the
eligible members of the Baseball Writers' Association of
America to elect Stengel. The vote was unanimous.

It was the result of this voting which was announced at
Huggins-Stengel Field that day. Ford C. Frick, then just re-
cently retired as Commissioner of Baseball, walked up to
the microphone before an overflow crowd. "A special election has been held," Frick said, "and Charles Dillon
Stengel has been unanimously elected to the Hall of
Fame."

Just before Frick made the announcement, a wry smile
crossed Stengel's face and there remains the suspicion that
he had guessed what was up. Once the word was out, pandemonium broke loose and Stengel was caught a little short
for words, if such a thing is really possible. But he recovered well and began a response to the news after an im-
pulsive kiss from Edna who was carrying an immense spray
of roses which had been ordered for the erstaz "presentation."

When the news of Stengel's election into the Hall of
Fame was announced, reaction was understandbly favorable, even from some old adversaries.

"I've never met a man more devoted to baseball,"
Ralph Houk, Stengel's successor as manager of the
Yankees was to say that March day from the Yankees'
camp at Ft. Lauderdale. "All he ever cared to talk about
was baseball, day or night, on the field or in a hotel lobby.
If we were to meet right this minute, we'd start talking
baseball."

"That's a wonderful and important thing. It's one of
the things that made him an outstanding manager, because
that's passed on to ballplayers. You think about it and you
come to understand more.

"We all know what his record was as Yankee manager,
so I don't have to repeat that. But how long was he in
baseball? 55 years? Think of that and all he ever did was
enhance it."

Gil Hodges, later to lead the Mets to a World Championship had closed his playing career at the Polo Grounds under Stengel. He was then managing the Washington Senators and was at their training base in Pompano Beach.

"It's great," said Hodges. "No man deserved it more. He has been such great public relations for baseball and knows so much about it and had such a fine record. I appreciated him much more when I was around him than I ever could in the slight contact we had with him as an opponent in the World Series when I was with the Dodgers.

"It's hard to pin down what you learned from a man— it's an interaction of personalities. I may take away one thing while PeeWee Reese or Duke Snider might get something else, whether it's from Leo Durocher or Charlie Dressen or Stengel or any other manager.

"But I feel a lot of his influence rubbed off on me. He was around so long, he knew so much, he noticed everything—and there were things about handling men, which is an important part of managing, in which he helped me."

Even from baseball men who had never played for or with Stengel came high praise. Bobby Bragan, one-time National League catcher and later president of the Texas League, had managed against Stengel in the majors. He said, "I'm delighted. Stengel has meant as much to baseball as Babe Ruth in making people think and talk about it. But the outstanding thing he brings to my mind is longevity as a manager. He proved it and longevity is a subject dear to the hearts of managers."

Accolades were both universal and well-deserved. But it was a long way from the end of the line for Casey.

Bragan's comment seemed somewhat extravagant in light of the commonly-held place of Babe Ruth above and beyond all other men in the baseball history books. Yet, it was pregnant with truth. Stengel's long career had shown him to be a wise user of publicity, comic and otherwise, to attract attention to baseball. He used all of the tools at his command to focus public notice to what his team was doing. Three of the four major league teams he managed were losers.

William D. Eckert, then the Commissioner, shook

Stengel's hand warmly and called it "a great day for baseball." Weiss, largely responsible for the altering of the voting rule, acknowledged that Stengel was on his mind when he suggested that a man over sixty-five should be eligible for election to permit "him to smell the flowers now."

Stengel responded to the announcement by saying, "I guess I should say a thousand things, being elected into the Hall of Fame is an amazing thing and there are so many men which are skilled in various ways. So many noted men have got into the Hall of Fame and I think it's a terrific thing to get in while you're still alive."

Edna Stengel, obviously thrilled, commented, "I can't get over it. This is greater even than winning the 1949 World Series."

Casey, hobbled by his hip injury and brandishing his black walking stick, then proceeded to cross the field from one side to the other and inform crowds in the bleacher sections on both sides, "They just put me in, if you didn't know, the Hall of Fame." Each repitition of the announcement was greeted by raucous cheers.

Thus thrust immediately back into the limelight on the first day of spring training the year following his retirement, Stengel picked right up where he had left off the previous year.

His induction ceremony on July 25 was the stage for another hilarious exposition of Stengelese which lasted for twenty-one minutes and turned the ceremonies into uproar.

The induction ceremony at Cooperstown was held on the site of what is now the National Baseball Library and served to reunite Stengel with one of his favorite opposing players—Ted Williams. Williams had been elected in the regular voting the previous year as the 103rd man in the Hall of Fame and thus shared the platform with Stengel when both were inducted.

During his commentary for the benefit of the press and the cameras that spring at St. Petersburg, Stengel had said, "I felt there was something wrong going on here when I see so many writers and cameramen. But I figger that we gotta do something like this to get Weiss which has been my amazin' friend for forty-five years when he owned the New

Haven ballclub and I was doin' my managing in the Eastern League. He had a higher education through Yale than I did and so I had to do all the talkin' while he was bringing in the ballplayers. It's gotta be a great honor and this and that. A lotta great men and it's sad to know fellas like Rube Marquard, him with the crocked neck, would say, 'I'd like to get into that thing; him that win 20 straight games. I'll be goin' in the Hall of Fame with Williams which I never got out in four years. If I still have this cane, I'll hook him around the neck with it when I see him at Cooperstown.''

Stengel didn't have to do any guessing about what was going to happen when he went to Cooperstown, but, contrary to his spring remarks, he didn't wrap his cane around Ted Williams' neck.

On the contrary, Williams and Stengel became a great act.

Yet the Brooklyn Dodgers, Boston Braves and New York Mets were almost constantly the recipients of favorable press during his years as their field manager.

With the Mets, in particular, his role was performed with spectacular results. One of the worst teams ever assembled, playing in an abandoned ballpark in a hotly competitive market, the Mets became virtually dominant on the sports pages in New York. It was, of course, partly due to their role as the city's only National League entry after decades of the Giants and Dodgers. Most early Met fans were from the residue of the two earlier teams and their allegiance to the National League was powerful. But it was Stengel who galvanized that allegiance into paid attendance with a team which was, frankly, disgraceful.

There was some irony to the induction into the Hall of Fame in that it was Williams with whom Stengel shared the podium, if, indeed, Stengel ever shared a podium with anyone. It is more likely that he merely lent it to them for awhile before or after his turn to speak came. Nobody ever successfully topped Casey Stengel at a baseball affair as a public speaker. Few even attempted it.

But in Williams, Stengel had a partner whom he truly admired. Much of the admiration was rooted in Stengel's observance of Williams as one of the great hitters in the history of baseball and, without doubt, the best pure hitter in the game since the 1930s. But one incident cemented the bond between the two men and led Stengel to regard Williams with the highest personal regard.

With all of the success Stengel achieved while managing the Yankees and the club's sensational record in World Series play, Casey was never able to consistently win All-Star Games against the National League and, in fact, it was during Stengel's years that the American League began its decline in the mid-summer series.

But Williams was a favorite of Stengel's for having given literally his all in an effort to win Casey's first All-Star effort and endangering his career in the process. It was 1950 when Stengel, by virtue of the 1949 A.L. pennant, managed his first All-Star at Chicago's Comiskey Park.

In the first inning, Williams rammed into the concrete leftfield wall at Comiskey snagging a drive off the bat of Ralph Kiner, the feared Pittsburgh Pirate slugger. Williams collided with the wall at full tilt and when he returned to the bench, Stengel asked, "You all right?" Williams said yes, but wasn't telling even close to the truth. His left elbow was nearly shattered and had begun to puff and discolor.

Williams was due to hit again in the fifth inning and Stengel observed him wincing while swinging a bat.

"Maybe you better sit it out, Ted," Stengel said.

"No, Case," Williams replied, "let me go to bat once more and see if I can hit."

Williams did bat and did hit, singling in the third American League run of the game which stood up for a 3-3 lead until the ninth when Kiner's homer tied it. After eight innings, Williams finally gave in to the pain and left the lineup.

In the 14th inning, Red Schoendienst of the Cardinals smacked a homer which gave the National League a 4−3 victory.

But the next day, Ted Williams was lying in a hospital operating room for more than one and a quarter hours while delicate surgery was performed on his elbow for the removal of seven bone chips. He missed nearly half a season as a result.

Even after he was past his prime and no longer a starting regular in the All-Star balloting, Williams was a member of every All-Star squad Stengel ever assembled.

"I ain't ever gonna leave out the fella which once played eight innings for me with a broken arm and also got himself a hit. Amazin'." Stengel never forgot.

Even before their joint induction into the Hall of Fame, Williams and Stengel were reunited by baseball. The 1966 All-Star Game was played in St. Louis and the pair, as future inductees into the Hall of Fame, were honored as part of the pre-game ceremonies. As usual, Stengel stole the show.

The various vocal pyrotechnics surrounding Casey's induction into the Hall of Fame were really an extension of the show which he had been putting on for over five decades in pro baseball.

As early as 1911, as a minor league outfielder, he exhibited his clown instincts by climbing into a drainage culvert buried in leftfield and emerged just in time to snag a fly ball for an out. His manager, Kid Elberfeld, a former Yankee skipper, failed to be amused.

One of the greatest vocal performances in the history of Western man was probably presented by Stengel when he faced the power of the United States Senate in 1958. The Kefauver committee considering some anti-trust legislation that related to baseball, collected several star players (including Ted Williams, Stan Musial and Mickey Mantle) amongst its witnesses. They also called Professor Stengel.

In response to a question from Sen. Kefauver as to why baseball might want the bill passed, Stengel offered the following:

"Well, I would have to say at the present time, I think, that baseball has advanced in this respect for the player help. That is an amazing statement for me to make because you can retire with an annuity at 50 and what organization in America allows you to retire at 50 and receive money?

"I want to further state that I am not a ball player, that is, put into that pension fund committee. At my age, and I have been in baseball, well, I say I am possibly the oldest man who is working in baseball. I would say that when they start an annuity for the ball players to better their conditions, it should have been done, and I think it has been done.

"I think it should be the way they have done it, which is a very good thing.

"The reason they possibly did not take the managers in at that time was because radio and television or the income to the ballclubs was not large enough that you could have put in a pension plan.

"Now I am not a member of the pension plan. You have young men here who are, who represent the ball clubs.

"They represent the players and since I am not a member and don't receive pension from a fund which you think, my goodness, he ought to be declared in that, too, but I would say that is a great thing for the ball players.

"That is one thing I will say for the ball players they have an advanced pension fund. I should think it was gained by radio and television or you could not have enough money to pay anything of that type.

"Now the second thing about baseball that I think is very interesting to the public or to all of us that it is the owner's own fault if he does not improve his club, along with the officials in the ball clubs and the players.

"Now what causes that?"

"If I am going to go on the road and we are a travelling ball club and you know the cost of transportation now—we travel sometimes with three Pullman coaches, the New York Yankees, and remember I am just a salaried man and do not own stock in the New York Yankees. I found out that in traveling with the New York Yankees on the road and all, that it is the best, and we have broken records in Washington this year, we have broken them in every city but New York and we have lost two clubs that have gone out of the city of New York."

"Of course, we have had some bad weather, I would say that they are mad at us in Chicago, we fill the parks.

"They have come out to see good material, I will say they are mad at us in Kansas City, but we broke the attendance record.

"Now on the road we only get possibly 27 cents. I am not positive of these figures, as I am not an official.

"If you go back 15 years or if I owned stock in the club I would give them to you."

Kefauver then said, "I am not sure that I made my question clear." This brought on a round of laughter from the packed hearing room.

"Yes, sir," Stengel replied, "Well, that is all right. I am not sure I am going to answer yours perfectly, either." More laughter.

"I was asking you, sir," Kefauver pressed on, "why is it that baseball wants this bill passed?"

Stengel then continued, "I would say I would not know, but I would say the reason why they want it passed is to keep baseball going as the highest paid ball sport that has gone into baseball and from the baseball angle, I am not going to speak of any other sport."

"I am not in here to argue about other sports, I am in the baseball business. It has been run cleaner than any business that was ever put out in the 100 years at the present time.

"I am not speaking about television or I am not speaking about income that comes into the ball parks. You have to take that off. I don't know too much about it. I say the ball players have a better advancement at the present time. . . ."

Kefauver surrendered gracefully and yielded to his fellow Senator, "Very well . . . Senator Langer?"

Senator Langer than inquired as to whether baseball would expand with more major league teams.

"I think," said Stengel, "every chamber of commerce in the major league cities would not change a franchise. I think they will be delighted because they have a hard time to put in a convention hall or to let people to come to your city and if it is going to be like Milwaukee or Kansas City or Baltimore, I think they would want a major league team."

Langer's next question was whether the Yankee owners could sell to someone without consent of the other American League clubs.

Stengel's answer was, "That is a very good thing that I will have to think about but I will give you an example.

"I think that is why they put in as a commissioner Judge Landis, and he said if there is a cloud on baseball I will take it off and he took the cloud off and they have only had one scandal or if they had it is just one major league city.

"How can you be a ball player and make 25 ball players framed with it being heard?

"It is bound to leak, and your play will show it.

"I don't think an owner possible could do something but he can't play the game for you. It is the most honest profession I think that we have, everything today that is going on outside . . . "

Senator Langer, then catching the spirit of the thing, asked:

"I want to know whether you intend to keep on monopolizing the world's championship in New York City?"

"Well, I will tell you," Stengel was off again, "I got a little concern yesterday in the first three innings when I say the three players I had gotten rid of and I said when I lost nine what am I going to do, and when I had a couple of my players, I thought so great of that did not do so good up to the sixth inning, I was more confused but I finally had to go and call on a young man in Baltimore that we don't own and the Yankees don't own him, and he is doing pretty good, and I would actually have to tell you that I think we are more the Greta Garbo type now from success."

The other questions and answers went along more-or-less in the same vein, leaving the audience convulsed with laughter and the Senate Anti-Trust and Monopoly Subcommittee in disarray. Stengel addressed the Senators for over three-quarters of an hour and used over 7,000 words in the English language. At no point did he ever address himself to the legislation being considered and he never rendered an answer to any question of consequence. Yet, he was clearly the star of the entire proceeding.

Following his testimony, *The Sporting News* headlined its story on the hearings: "Casey was Eloquent, but What Did He Say?"

It remained for Mickey Mantle to deliver the crushing blow to the Senators when, in response to one of their questions, he answered, "My views are about the same as Casey's." The laughter was heard all the way to the White House.

Stengel was, of course, more than capable of giving a direct answer to a direct question when he wished to do so. He was in reality following some public relations advice he had gotten decades before when he assumed his first big league managerial post at Brooklyn. Ring Lardner, the fabled baseball writer, author and man of letters, told him to just keep talking and the press would get a story somewhere, somehow. Lardner was right and Stengel proved it.

He also knew that his employment of Stengelese would enable him to evade responding to any question which he didn't really want to answer and mask his real intentions when questioned about things he really didn't want to discuss. Yet, he always produced answers which could, if the occasion demanded, be used even if only for the purpose of illustrating what a character Casey Stengel was. If that was the sole result, Casey was satisfied with it.

The peculiar syntax and rambling dialogues also made him distinctive and this was another value from Stengel's point of view. As a result, he became the most quoted and most famous spokesman for the game of baseball for almost four decades, all of that following his retirement as an active player. No man in any line of endeavor will probably ever be able to match his achievement in that regard. Stengel was an excellent manager who always got out of his material whatever it had to give and could win when he had the guns. There have been other men in baseball who could do the same thing, although not as many as may be thought. But Stengel was unparalleled in his public relations sense and his ability to generate personal publicity.

The fact that his monologues often resembled both sides of the conversation between the walrus and the carpenter was something far from accidental.

In 1969, when the Mets had won their first pennant ever but had not yet begun the World Series against Baltimore (which they were also to win), *The New York Times* deputized sportswriter Joe Durso to interview Stengel via telephone. The conversation opened with Durso asking Stengel if Casey thought the Mets were still "splendid and fairly amazin'" to which Stengel responded:

"Yes, yes, yes, oh yes, yes. There's nothing wrong with what they've done. I'm very proud to see them improving so well, and you'd have to say that Seaver is an outstanding pitcher, he went to U.S.C. university you know. I've been looking for the club to improve itself and you could see in spring training that they commenced to come around.

"You take Cleon Jones, which was a fairly timid player once, and the centerfielder can throw for distance now. Out here he stood near the centerfield fence and threw the ball to home plate 400 and something feet and they're both from Mobile besides. And now they make the cutoff play, which keeps the other fellow from taking two bases. But now they can do it in right-center and left-center, too; where you used to make mistakes, and besides they're especially good on ground balls.

I'd have to say the manager has got six or seven out-fielders and six men who can hit the ball a distance and Jones also led the club in stolen bases (actually, Agee led the Mets in 1969 with 26 steals, ed.), which he is—a base stealer."

'And the other man, Agee, can run from first base to second. You could look it up, the manager did a tremen-dous job, and he brought the coaches with him, too, and Berra was a very honest player besides. I could go to him in a meeting and he would probably see you could get this man out with this pitch, and he was very honest in his answers, and so Raschi and Reynolds became terrific pitchers, and Lopat could throw the changeup or anything and Berra would catch the ball."

Durso then asked Stengel how he would compare his Mets (vintage 1962-65) with the pennant-winning team.

"Well, in Florida they built four baseball parks and called it a complex, and the quickest man they got educated is, you'd have to say, Seaver. In the game between the two leagues (the All-Star Game) out here at Anaheim, his first year in the big league, he got the man out and he's been cor-recting his weaknesses rapidly. And so the other players start following him around and copying him and the second pitcher, I'd have to say, is Koosman and the third is McGraw, which throws a very fast ball.

"They also have six men who can run now, and the catcher's done a terrific job. So the other men on the other clubs are afraid to run. He doesn't allow the pitcher to commence worrying about the runner because he's got an amazing arm. Now with all of the young pitchers, that's important, and besides with a complex down there they can slides and if you can't field the ball, they'll show you why not. And so they put 50 or so men in spring training and commenced to improve, and the public is sticking with them."

When asked his opinion of the upcoming World Series against Baltimore, Stengel said:

"I saw Baltimore win four in a row (1966 vs. the Dodgers) and he's got some pretty good players, and we lost the centerfielder (Paul Blair, the Oriole star, was a former Met). He's got four or five pitchers which can get a man out if he can throw the ball over the plate. You will find that their jumps—what you would call an inch or more. If you sit behind home plate or sit and watch television, the ball jumps, and a good pitching staff is the biggest thing in baseball. So if the Mets don't blow it, they can continue a month more."

As subsequent events proved, they didn't blow it, knocking out the Orioles in five games by winning the last four in a row.

Durso then ventured into a comparison between Casey's original Mets and the 1969 edition. Stengel produced the following in response:

"Yes, it used to be we'd run everybody out of Buffalo because they couldn't play, and you couldn't send the high-priced players there anyway. And we beat the Cardinals two days that year but not the last day, and then you would've had a triple tie, and people ask how can you have a triple tie? St. Louis kept on winning in the World Series, and this club can, too. We used to get run out of the towns we played in, but New York stayed by them and I'm proud of them all.

"This here club doesn't make many mistakes now, you can see they believe in each other, and the coaches all live in New York and you can get them on the phone.

"So I'm very proud of these fellows, which did such a splendid job, and if they can keep improving like this, they can keep going till Christmas."

The Mets didn't exactly keep going until Christmas, because, even by Stengel standards, it gets a little cold in New York for baseball on Christmas. But, in 1973, with immortal Willie Mays added to the cast as a spot player, the Mets did win another pennant and eliminated favored Cincinnati in the National League playoffs. Then followed a World Series packed with the bizarre incidents for which the Mets are famous. Mays drove in the decisive run in a wild game at Oakland and A's owner Charlie Finley "fired" second baseman Mike Andrews for making two errors in one inning. Baseball commissioner Bowie Kuhn then "unfired" Andrews. The Mets battled Oakland through an exciting 7-game Series before the A's finally won it.

The following year, Stengel was hospitalized briefly and upon his discharge announced to the awaiting world that he had been suffering from a severe throat infection.

"The doctors say I ain't allowed to talk," Casey reported.

He took off from the point into a lengthly description of the disorder which afflicted him and then carried on another half hour about his 55-year career in baseball. Stengel was always one for confounding the medical experts as well as the baseball ones. But in early 1975, the curtain began to come down on the Stengel saga. Early in the year, Edna suffered a stroke and was hospitalized.

She was subsequently confined to a nursing home.

In mid-September, Stengel himself entered Glendale Memorial Hospital for tests. When he had last appeared in New York on June 28 for the Mets' Old Timers' Day ceremonies at Shea Stadium, Casey was asked about his trip from Glendale to New York. He replied, "Don't ask about my trip, ask about my body." Later on during the season, Stengel skipped the Yankees' Old Timer festivities and announced that he probably would not attend any more of the nostalgia days which had become major staging areas for his performance since his retirement as Mets' manager in 1965.

The tests indicated that Stengel was a victim of malignant sarcona, a form of cancer which affects the lymph glands and was centered in the abdomen.

At 1:58 A.M., New York time, on September 30, Casey Stengel succumbed to the disease.

The reaction to his passing was immediate, immense, sincere and moving.

"Casey Stengel was not a man. He was a presence," wrote Maury Allen in the *New York Post*, "He was a force of energy, a happening, a steamroller of excitement and vigor.

"He loved life. He loved it with a passion that consumed him. He loved laughter. He loved the game of baseball.

"Stengel had a massive ego. There were tons of ham in him. His style upset the stuffed shirts, the pompous, the phonies. He was a man who engendered violent reaction. Hate him with a passion, as many did like Howard Cosell, Phil Rizzuto, Jerry Coleman and Joe DiMaggio, or love him, as most newspapermen around him did. Never, never ignore him. He didn't die from cancer. He died because people started ignoring him at 85. He couldn't take that."

Rod Dedeaux, baseball coach at Southern California, a former player for Stengel at Brooklyn, and one of the aging Casey's closest friends, visited him in the hospital the night before he died. Owing to Edna's incapacitation, Dedeaux handled most of the arrangements following Casey's death. He was to find that many of those who had disagreed with Stengel and even fought with him over the years really didn't hate him, either, as might have been commonly thought.

The messages concerning Stengel's death came from friend and foe in baseball and out.

Dedeaux himself commented, "I would say that baseball has lost absolutely the greatest manager it ever had. He was one of the most universally beloved men in all sports history and made great contributions to the game."

"It's just impossible to sum up what he's been to our game," said Harry Dalton, general manager of the California Angels, "I think he popularized our game with so many people. I think his common appeal as a character made him something of a latter-day Dizzy Dean to everyone attracted to our game."

"Casey Stengel was Mr. Baseball all the years I've

known him. I know he'll be missed both on and off the
field," said Buzzy Bavasi, the former Dodger executive
then president of the Padres."

New York Mayor Abraham Beame was quoted,
"Casey will always enjoy a special niche in the hearts of
New Yorkers. For it was at Ebbets Field that Casey
managed the old Brooklyn Dodgers and it was at Yankee
Stadium that Casey reached his greatest triumphs as
manager of the Yankees. And it was in New York, too, less
than 10 miles away at Shea Stadium that the ever-popular
Casey nudged his way even deeper into the hearts of the
unpredicable New York baseball fans by finishing 10th
every year he managed our beloved Mets. I, along with
millions of his fans, will sorely miss him."

Stengel, having been a player and manager for the
Dodgers, a player for the Giants, a manager for the
Yankees and manager of the Mets, was distinguished as the
only man ever to wear the uniform of all four New York
major league baseball teams which operated in the 20th century.

"There has never been anyone like him and never can
be," said Commissioner Kuhn. "Casey was irrepressibly
himself. But Casey left a nation that adored him and a host
of memories so vivid and marvelous that we really can't
ever lose him."

Gabe Paul, president of the Yankees, made some ob-
servations concerning those who played for Stengel on the
Yankees, as well as adding his own comments on his passing. "He enjoyed life to its fullest and all those who came
into contact with him were inspired by his perpetual youth.
Of the Yankee players he managed, six became big-league
managers, eleven became coaches, six became scouts,
three became broadcasters, six became college baseball
coaches and two became baseball executives. There's a
great deal of Casey Stengel left in baseball."

Many of those players were also heard from:

Yogi Berra said, "Baseball lost a great man. If he
wanted to make sense, he could. When you got him to talk
about baseball, he made a lot of sense."

"The Stengel era was on unto itself," Elston Howard
said, "I can't say enough about him because of what he did

for me. I was the first black player signed (by the Yankees) and he made breaching the color line easier for me. He told hotel managers he would not allow the team to stay if I wasn't welcome, too.''

'Stengel had a unique technique of two-platooning his men. He worked guys like myself, Mickey Mantle, Bobby Richardson and Tony Kubek gradually until we became major leaguers. And this way he carried a continuous supply of good talent.''

Mantle, one of the great players closest to Stengel during his years with the Yankees, said simply, ''He was like a father to me.''

Joe DiMaggio, about whom it was often said he and Stengel mutually disagreed, somewhat surprised many people with the warmth and sincerity of his tribute. ''He was wonderful, he understood his players and he knew what to do with the talent he had.''

New York's govenor Carey said, ''Casey Stengel had the baseball mind of a genius, the heart of Santa Claus and St. Francis, and the face of a clown, and something very good has gone from our lives.

''Casey Stengel will be ranked in the history of baseball with such great managers as John McGraw, Connie Mack and Joe McCarthy. And New Yorkers will always hold him in their hearts with warm memory. He made a unique contribution, too, to American letters with his inimitable 'Stengelese,' a language for which he invented his own prose and syntax. He was a joy in more ways than anyone in public life. We shall not see his like again.''

Mr. Donald Grant, chairman of the board of the Mets, released a statement which read:

''Casey Stengel proved himself to be the most romantic figure in the history of baseball. It is a great personal loss to everyone associated with the Mets from groundskeepers to Mrs. Payson (Joan Whitney Payson, owner of the Mets who was herself to die a few days later) and, in fact, everyone who ever saw a baseball game.''

Funeral services for Casey Stengel were held on October 6 at the Church of the Recessional in Forest Lawn Memorial Park in Glendale.

Among those who served as honorary pallbearers for

their former leader were ex-players Billy Martin, Charlie
Silvera, Irv Noren, Tom Morgan and Jerry Coleman.
Others in attendance included former Met Rod Kanehl, a
Stengel favorite, and Babe Herman, former famous out-
fielder at Brooklyn, Fred Haney and Jocko Conlan.

Baseball's heirarchy also turned out in force.

On hand were Commissioner Kuhn, American League
president Lee MacPhail, Giant owner Horace Stoneham,
Met general manager Joe McDonald, Padre president
Buzzy Bavasi, California Angel president Red Patterson,
and others.

Kuhn and Dedeaux both delivered eulogies.

Kuhn said, in part, "No one has a greater debt to
Casey Stengel than baseball. When you think of all the
things he could have been, and been outstanding at, to have
him 100 percent in baseball was a wonderful thing for us.
He helped us not to take ourselves too seriously. He made
more fans for baseball than any other man who ever lived."

The funeral was also heavily attended by Stengel's
friends, neighbors, baseball fans, older residents of the
Glendale area and teenage boys familiar with him and his
work with youth baseball programs.

The services were marred somewhat by rain, but it remained for Dedeaux to close the activities on the most
proper note. Quoting a newspaper column written when
Stengel died, Dedeaux said, "Well, God is certainly getting
an earful tonight."

Appendix One

Casey Stengel's Record as a Player

b., July 30, 1889 (Kansas City, Mo.)
d., September 30, 1975 (Glendale, Calif.)

Year	Club	League	Gms	Hits	HR	RBI	B.A.
1910	Kansas City[1]	A.A.	—	—	—	—	—
1910	Kankakee[2]	Northern	—	—	—	—	—
1910	Maysville	Blue Grass	69	52	2	—	.223
1911	Aurora	Wisc.-Ill.	121	148	4	—	*.352
1912	Montgomery	Southern	136	139	—	—	.290
1912	Brooklyn	N.L.	17	18	1	12	.316
1913	Brooklyn	N.L.	124	119	7	44	.272
1914	Brooklyn	N.L.	126	130	4	56	.279
1915	Brooklyn	N.L.	132	109	3	43	.237
1916	Brooklyn	N.L.	127	129	8	53	.279
1917	Brooklyn[3]	N.L.	150	141	6	69	.257
1918	Pittsburgh[4]	N.L.	39	30	1	13	.246
1919	Pittsburgh[5]	N.L.	89	94	4	40	.293
1920	Philadelphia	N.L.	129	130	9	50	.292
1921	Philadelphia[6]	N.L.	24	18	0	5	.305
1921	N.Y. Giants	N.L.	18	5	0	1	.227
1922	N.Y. Giants	N.L.	84	92	7	48	.368
1923	N.Y. Giants[7]	N.L.	75	74	5	43	.339
1924	Boston	N.L.	131	129	5	39	.280
1925	Boston[8]	N.L.	12	1	0	2	.077
1925	Worcester	Eastern	100	107	10	—	.320
1926	Toledo	A.A.	88	66	0	27	.328

1927 Toledo ..............A.A.	18	3	1	3	.176
1928 Toledo ..............A.A.	26	14	0	12	.438
1929 Toledo ..............A.A.	20	7	0	9	.226
1930 Toledo ..............A.A.	—	—	—	—	—
1931 Toledo ..............A.A.	2	3	0	0	.375
Major league totals	1277	1219	60	518	.284

[1]Signed but did not play; optioned to Kankakee

[2]League folded in mid-season, no records kept

[3]Traded Jan. 9, 1918, to Pittsburgh with second baseman George Cutshaw for infielder Chuck Ward, pitchers Burleigh Grimes and Al Mamaux

[4]In U.S. Navy most of season

[5]Traded to Philadelphia, August, 1919, for outfielder George Whitted; refused to report to Phillies in salary dispute and sat out balance of season

[6]Traded to New York Giants, July, 1921, for players valued at $75,000

[7]Traded to Boston Braves, Nov., 1923, with shortstop Dave Bancroft and outfielder Billy Cunningham for pitcher Joe Oeschger and outfielder Billy Southworth

[8]Named president, general manager and playing manager of Worcester when Boston (NL) purchased club, May 22, 1925

World Series Playing Record

Year	Club	Gms	AB	R	H	2B	3B	HR	RBI	B.A.
1916	Brooklyn-NL	4	11	2	4	0	0		0	0	.364
1922	New York-NL	2	15	0	2	0	0		0	0	.400
1923	New York-NL	6	12	3	5	0	0		2	4	.417
	World Series totals	12	28	5	11	0	0		2	4	.393

Appendix Two

Stengel's Records as a Manager

Year	Team	League	Won	Lost	Position
1925	Worcester[1]	Eastern	70	55	4th
1926	Toledo	American Assn.	87	77	4th
1927	Toledo	American Assn.	101	67	1st
1928	Toledo	American Assn.	79	88	6th
1929	Toledo	American Assn.	67	100	8th
1930	Toledo	American Assn.	88	66	3rd
1931	Toledo	American Assn.	68	100	7th
1934	Brooklyn[2]	National	71	81	6th
1935	Brooklyn	National	70	83	5th
1936	Brooklyn	National	67	87	7th
1938	Boston	National	77	75	5th
1939	Boston	National	63	88	7th
1940	Boston	National	65	87	7th
1941	Boston	National	62	92	7th
1942	Boston	National	59	89	7th
1943	Boston	National	68	85	6th
1944	Milwaukee[3]	American Assn.	91	49	1st
1945	Kansas City	American Assn.	65	86	7th
1946	Oakland	Pacific Coast	111	72	2nd
1947	Oakland	Pacific Coast	96	90	4th
1948	Oakland	Pacific Coast	114	74	1st
1949	New York	American	97	57	1st
1950	New York	American	98	56	1st
1951	New York	American	98	56	1st
1952	New York	American	95	59	1st
1953	New York	American	99	52	1st
1954	New York	American	103	51	2nd
1955	New York	American	96	58	1st

1956 New York	.... American	97	57	1st
1957 New York	.... American	98	56	1st
1958 New York	.... American	92	62	1st
1959 New York	.... American	79	75	3rd
1960 New York[4]	.... American	97	57	1st
1962 New York	.... National	40	120	10th
1963 New York	.... National	51	111	10th
1964 New York	.... National	53	109	10th
1965 New York[5]	.... National ...,..	31	64	10th

Notes

1—Took over club May 22, 1925, with team in eighth place.

2—Replaced Max Carey for 1934 season, served as coach for Brooklyn, 1932-33.

3—Replaced Charlie Grimm May 5, 1944, with team in first place.

4—Dismissed October 18, 1960.

5—Replaced by Wes Westrum, July 25, 1965, after injury to hip.

World Series Managing Record

(All series with New York Yankees)

Year	Opponent	Result
1949	Brooklyn	Won, 4-1
1950	Philadelphia	Won, 4-0
1951	New York Giants	Won, 4-2
1952	Brooklyn	Won, 4-3
1953	Brooklyn	Won 4-2
Year	Opponent	Result
1955	Brooklyn	Lost, 4-3
1956	Brooklyn	Won, 4-3
1957	Milwaukee	Lost, 4-3
1958	Milwaukee	Won, 4-3
1960	Pittsburgh	Lost, 4-3

Copy 1   B
                                          Stengel
MacLean, Norman
  Casey Stengel.

                                             $9.95